Praise for Light and Death

In this insightful and very valuable contribution, Dr. Sabom scrutinizes the NDEs of Christians through the lenses of both science and Scripture. He offers a compelling and plausible perspective, which not only makes sense of a lot of contradictory evidence, but also helps to explain why NDEs often convey such a mixed spiritual message.

Elizabeth L. Hillstrom, Ph.D.
Associate Professor of Psychology, Wheaton College
Author of *Testing the Spirits*

Dr. Sabom clearly argues that the NDE is not an experience of the afterlife but a confirmation of its reality. Using Scripture, he exhorts us to trust only in Jesus Christ, the light of life and lover of our souls.

Kelly Monroe
Editor of *Finding God at Harvard:
Spiritual Journals of Thinking Christians*

Dr. Sabom provides us with a needed scientific look at near-death experiences under the scrutiny of God's holy Word, the Bible, the only reliable source of eternal truth. The results of his study are truly fascinating.

Dr. Bill Bright, Founder and President
Campus Crusade for Christ International

Praise for Dr. Sabom's research and Recollections of Death

The kind of work Sabom is doing, and the integrity with which he is doing it, indicates that it is time for him to be joined by other Christian physicians and scientists.

Richard Abanes
Author of *Embraced by the Light and the Bible*

To my knowledge, the only truly objective study of adult near-death experiences is the one done by Atlanta cardiologist Michael Sabom.

Melvin Morse, M.D.
Author of *Transformed by the Light*

The research of Michael Sabom deserves special attention. Although his book, *Recollections of Death*, is presently out of print, it probably presents the most objective observations on the near-death experience.

J. Isamu Yamamoto
Christian Research Journal

... [Sabom's study] has become a benchmark in the field of near-death research.

Raymond Moody, M.D., Ph.D.
Author of *Life After Life*

One of the most cautious, and therefore most startling, studies of out-of-body experiences during near-death experiences was conducted by Dr. Michael Sabom ... who is one of the leading researchers in the near-death field.

Mally Cox-Chapman
Author of *The Case for Heaven*

Recollections of Death is a sober book, eschewing both religious and science fiction. ... From a theological point of view, there is nothing incongruous in the general characteristics of the near-death experience as described by Sabom. ... This is just what one would expect ... as the soul becomes more knowing as death approaches.

P. H. Hallett
National Catholic Register

Probably the most impressive study of the NDE's paranormal features was made by Dr. Michael Sabom in the 1970s. ... [I]t extended the scientific study of the NDE in entirely new directions.

D. Scott Rogo
Author of *The Return from Silence*

While his overall findings are in accord with Ring's study, Sabom's book is distinguished by the care that he took to provide independent corroborative evidence for the visual and auditory perceptions reported by near-death survivors when allegedly out of the body, so that his research data strongly support the claims made by his respondents.

Margot Grey
Author of *Return from Death*

LIGHT & DEATH

One Doctor's Fascinating Account of Near-Death Experiences

MICHAEL SABOM, M.D.

ZondervanPublishingHouse

Grand Rapids, Michigan

A Division of HarperCollinsPublishers

Light and Death
Copyright © 1998 by Michael Sabom

Requests for information should be addressed to:

ZondervanPublishingHouse
Grand Rapids, Michigan 49530

Library of Congress Cataloging-in-Publication Data

Sabom, Michael B.
  Light and death : one doctor's fascinating account of near-death expeiences / Michael Sabom.
      p.   cm.
  Includes bibliographical references.
  ISBN 0-310-21992-2 (pbk. : alk. paper)
  1. Near-death experiences.   2. Near-death experiences—Religious aspects—Christianity.   I. Title.
BF1045.N4S23 1998
133.9'01'3—dc21   98-41357
                                                                      CIP

Interior design by Sherri L. Hoffman

Printed in the United States of America

---

98 99 00 01 02 03 04 05 /❖ DC/ 10 9 8 7 6 5 4 3 2

To Diane and Shay,
two lights in my life

Contents

reface

It has been over fifteen years since I completed my first study of near-death experiences and wrote *Recollections of Death*. During this time, I have been immersed in the day-to-day demands of a busy medical practice and able, for the most part, to follow from the sidelines the debates and controversies which have grown up around this intriguing phenomenon. Four years ago, I reentered the field of NDE research to conduct The Atlanta Study, which extends my original findings in three directions—scientifically, by exploring the nature of the near-death experience as a spiritual and physical event and considering its relationship to the moment of death; medically, by examining its clinical effect on survival and healing; and theologically, by considering this experience in light of traditional Christian teaching.

The names in this book of the patients, doctors, and nurses in The Atlanta Study are fictitious except for Darrell Pell, Alison Pell, and Dr. Robert Spetzler. The medical details, however, are accurate, and the testimonies have been meticulously reconstructed from tape-recorded interviews. Whereas I bring my own faith into the book, I do not assume the reader shares in this faith.

The completion of this research and the writing of this book was a team effort. One hundred and sixty persons graciously consented to be interviewed and evaluated, with "Pam Reynolds" and Darrell Pell deserving special credit in this regard.

Stephen M. Miller assisted in organizing the structure of the book, in interviewing subjects in one of the stories, and in writing some of the material.

Calvin Edwards, president of *MainStream*Consulting in Atlanta, provided invaluable advice and direction. He is not only my agent, but also a close friend, a Christian brother, and a contributor to key sections of the book.

Drs. John Musselman, Quigg Lawrence, and John Gibbs critically read and improved the manuscript.

Dr. Robert Spetzler generously assisted by ensuring that my reconstruction of his surgical procedure on "Pam Reynolds" was accurate.

My editors, Lyn Cryderman and Rachel Boers, warmly welcomed me into the Zondervan family and patiently polished the pages which follow.

Members of East Cobb Presbyterian Church in Atlanta supported me throughout this process with prayer and encouragement. Pastors Dr. Rick Holmes and Stephen Jackson led me with wisdom through difficult theological concepts. Elders on the Session offered valuable critique. And my Home Fellowship Community prayed on a weekly basis for the Lord's guidance in this work. They include: Diane, Dianna, Hugh, Barb, Joe, Karen, Reg, Barbie, Judy, Bob, Ken H., Becky, Barbara, Jack, Adie, Chuck, Wendy, and Ken M.

My wife, Diane, has been my major source of ideas, editorial assistance, and encouragement. Without her love and steady reassurance this project would never have been completed.

Finally, the Head of the team, the Lord Jesus Christ, is my staff and my comforter. To him be all honor and glory.

It shouldn't shock the Christian when people undergoing clinical death and being revived come back with certain recollections. I've tried to keep an open mind, and I hope that this interesting phenomenon will get the benefit of further research, analysis, and evaluation. Too many of these experiences have been reported for us to simply dismiss them as imaginary or hoaxes.[1]

—DR. R. C. SPROUL
PROFESSOR OF SYSTEMATIC THEOLOGY
REFORMED THEOLOGICAL SEMINARY

One

THE ATLANTA STUDY:

A Second Look at the Near-Death Experience

Pete Morton, a 53-year-old Air Force veteran, climbed into the military-issue hospital chair the way a cowboy mounts a horse. Pete was a handsome, rugged-looking man with black hair, sun-browned skin, and a deep, raspy voice tinged with a Louisiana bayou drawl. He didn't look like a man in frail health. But he was. Sitting backward in the gray steel chair, he leaned his chest against the vinyl-padded backrest and lit up a cigarette. I still chuckle when I listen to the tape of my interview with him; you can hear him strike the match. I was his cardiologist. The year was 1977.

Pete had suffered two cardiac arrests several years earlier, and was resuscitated each time. Now he was complaining of chest pain. His physician had referred him to the Veteran's Administration hospital in Gainesville, Florida, for a heart catheterization— a procedure during which I would insert a nearly four-foot-long tube into one of his arteries and gently thread this tube through the artery into his heart. By using a dye injected through this tube, I would be able to clearly see in an X-ray video any heart damage or blockages that might be causing his pain.

Before I did the procedure, I needed to talk with Pete about his medical history. At the time, I was already a year into my research on near-death experiences (NDEs) in which I was asking resuscitated patients if they could remember anything unusual about their crisis.

When I asked Pete, the room fell silent. The only movement was a spiraling pillar of cigarette smoke rising and dispersing near the ceiling. Pete looked at the doorway behind me, I'm guessing to make sure no one else was around. As he finally began to speak, it was with embarrassing stammers. Clearly, I had caught him off guard. I was asking to hear about something he had told only to his wife, and, even to her, only in part. Once she had heard what little he was willing to say, she refused to let him speak of it again in her presence.

I assured Pete that he could talk freely with me and that I wouldn't think him crazy. I explained that I was researching the topic. He told me he had left his body during his first cardiac arrest and had watched the resuscitation. When I asked him to tell me what exactly he saw, he described the resuscitation with such detail and accuracy that I could have later used the tape to teach physicians.

Pete remembered seeing a doctor's first attempt to restore his heartbeat. "He struck me. And I mean he really whacked me. He came back with his fist from way behind his head and he hit me right in the center of my chest." Pete remembered them inserting a needle into his chest in a procedure that he said looked like "one of those Aztec Indian rituals where they take the virgin's heart out." He even remembered thinking that when they shocked him they gave him too much voltage. "Man, my body jumped about two feet off the table."

Before talking with Pete, and scores like him, I didn't believe there was such a thing as a near-death experience. I first heard of the near-death experience as I sat with 20 other people in the Seekers Sunday school class at Trinity United Methodist Church in Gainesville, Florida. Sarah Kreutziger, a psychiatric social worker, was giving a report on Raymond Moody's book *Life After Life,* a collection of stories about people who said they nearly died and who claimed to have seen the spiritual world. Some of these people said they had left their bodies and watched as doctors tried to save them.

In our classroom there was just one physician—me. Somebody asked what I thought.

"I don't believe it," I said.

That was my first public comment on near-death experiences.

As a doctor, I had witnessed and performed countless resuscitations. But never, ever, had a patient told me a story as bizarre as the stories Moody reported. And never had any of my colleagues spun such a yarn. I truly believed Raymond Moody was pulling a fast one.

Still, the Seekers class was so intrigued by his book, which seemed to reinforce belief in life after death, that they arranged for Sarah to present a report to all the adults in the church. Sarah asked me to serve as medical consultant for the session and to field any medical questions. I agreed reluctantly; I was convinced the topic was better suited to a barker outside a carnival sideshow.

To get ready for the presentation, Sarah and I each agreed to ask some of our patients if they had ever experienced anything like Moody described. I fully expected to collect several negative responses and return to church with my skepticism intact. My mentor, a gray-haired physician who was directing my final months of training in cardiology, assured me I would not be surprised. I believed him. He had an earned reputation as the consummate bedside physician; he knew his patients.

He was right. I was not surprised. Until patient number three.

I walked into Jane Stewart's room at about 8 P.M. on April 27, 1976. She was a 37-year-old housewife who lived in the suburbs of Orlando. Though she had come to the hospital for elective surgery, I saw on her medical history chart that she had almost died several times during her life—once with encephalitis as a child, once with toxemia during pregnancy, and once during gall bladder surgery.

When I asked Jane if she had had any unusual experiences during these brushes with death, the tone of her voice fell reverent.

Beneath her words rose powerful emotions. I became quickly aware that she was entrusting to me a story deeply personal. That story unfolded like the pages of Moody's book.

I was flabbergasted, but tried to maintain a sense of professionalism as I listened.

My colleague, Sarah, also found such a patient. At our church presentation, we each played excerpts of our taped interviews with these people.

You can read a book of stories about near-death experiences and walk away as skeptical as you were before you picked it up. But when you look into the eyes of an experiencer, and from four feet away watch the ebb and flow of authentic tears, your skepticism begins to wash away.

I started to believe there might be something to the stories that Moody reported. But all he had was a collection of stories; there was no science in his book. I decided to take the near-death experience to its next logical step—I wanted to see if it would pass scientific muster.

It did.

After five years of research, I published my findings in the book *Recollections of Death*. Perhaps the most startling discovery I made through my research was that, as many people came close to death, their essence, or spirit, actually seemed to leave their body. These people, like Pete Morton, saw details of their resuscitation that they could not otherwise have seen. One patient noticed the physician who failed to wear scuffs over his white, patent-leather shoes during open-heart surgery. In many cases I was able to confirm the patient's testimony with medical records and with hospital staff.

Skipping Religion

One thing I didn't do in my research was to give a second thought to religion. I allowed it no space in my book, no time in my lectures.

Why did I delve into the issue of immortality without taking my theology along? Frankly, I didn't see the point of wading into the religious implications of a bunch of stories that were unsubstantiated by even one scientific study.

The more embarrassing question is why I left the research scene after my work gave scientific credibility to the near-death experience. The answer is that I felt I had no more to say. I didn't have the spiritual insight at the time to see how much near-death stories could strengthen or undermine a person's religious faith. As a result, I let everyone draw their own conclusions from my work.

An attorney from Georgia wrote me. "You left your readers standing before the door of occult knowledge, saying, 'knock here if you wish.'"

I'm afraid he was right.

I had helped put the near-death experience on the scientific map. *Recollections of Death* was viewed as a landmark in the scientific documentation of near-death experiences. People fascinated with this new subject devoured it as it was translated into eight languages. But while I was looked to as a leader in the field, I left it to others—experiencers and researchers—to build theories about the spiritual meaning of this new information.

What followed was a firestorm of controversy.

People who said they had been to "the other side" began telling exactly what they had seen and learned there. Some of these incredibly detailed stories became best-selling books. Yet most of these books contained "revelations" that clashed with traditional Christian teaching—revelations that advocated consulting the dead, that taught reincarnation, and that assured us that absolutely everyone is going to heaven.

Many folks believed these stories were eyewitness reports from the afterlife. Other people warned that the Bible says Satan can disguise himself as an angel of light. Journalists argued that these stories were usually unsubstantiated. One best-selling author, for example, refused to provide medical documentation to support her claim that she died. The doctor of another best-selling writer said that some of the medical details crucial to her near-death experience "didn't happen."

The near absence of hellish stories provoked some Christians to accuse near-death experiencers as well as researchers—me included—of taking part in a "collusion" to deny the existence of hell. Some of the more notable researchers fired back, criticizing Christians for accepting only the NDEs that seemed to advance fundamentalist dogma. And Christians retaliated with charges that researchers and experiencers were doing exactly the same thing, but to advance Eastern and New Age philosophies.

As I have followed these arguments over the past decade, I have become increasingly disturbed about the direction NDE studies have taken. Of the hundreds of books, magazine articles, and other media reports on NDEs, only a handful contained scientific studies. And not one of these studies used the rigorous methodology of science to explore relationships between Christian beliefs and practices and the near-death experience.

In my clinical practice, I began asking my patients who reported having an NDE about how the experience had affected them, both spiritually and medically. What I began to hear in the clinic and at the hospital bedside left me baffled and intrigued.

The Faith Factor

According to media reports, near-death experiencers and researchers agreed that NDEs drew persons away from organized religion and toward a more abstract spirituality. But my observation from my own patients was exactly the opposite: NDEs seemed to produce a stronger faith and a higher level of commitment to traditional religious practice. Since much of the religious controversy surrounding the NDE hinged on this point, I was struck by this apparent contradiction.

In addition, I was intrigued with the possibility that this deepened faith and religious commitment in patients following an NDE could be affecting their medical outcome. Scientific studies were suggesting that a patient's depth of religious faith was a strong predictor of survival and healing in clinical situations. This possibility, however, had never been explored in NDE survivors.

Other medical studies, including one with seriously-ill cardiac patients in a major American hospital, had suggested that prayer was a major factor in survival and recovery. My patients were confiding in me that prayer had played an important role not only in their NDEs, but also in their healing. The effects of such prayer both by and for the near-death experiencer had, again, not been examined.

Finally, I continued to wonder just how near to death these people had really come. For more than two decades I had believed that NDEs were *near-death* experiences, not *after-death* experiences. As a result, I didn't think NDEs provided insights into life after death. Since the publication of *Recollections of Death*, however, new medical procedures were allowing doctors to bring people back from what had previously been defined as death. Could these new medical breakthroughs help our understanding of NDEs and death?

I decided to study these questions further. *This* time, I was determined to bring my theology along.

One patient in particular convinced me of how little I understood the deep spiritual meaning behind the near-death experience. I met this man one Saturday morning while I was making rounds at the hospital. He was critically ill and in the middle of 40 days and 40 nights of a dramatic medical and spiritual struggle. His name was Darrell Pell.

I will give you a new heart and put a new spirit in you; I will remove from you your heart of stone and give you a heart of flesh. And I will put my Spirit in you and move you to follow my decrees and be careful to keep my laws.

—Ezekiel 36:26–27

Two

DARRELL:

A Medical and Spiritual Change of Heart

Darrell Pell didn't realize he was having a cardiac arrest.

The 34-year-old grocery store manager was lying quietly in bed in the cardiac intensive care unit on the second floor of Saint Joseph's Hospital in Atlanta. He was there for a heart transplant. A nurse had stopped by and was chatting, as images flickered on the TV bolted to the top of the wall.

From outside the room and 15 paces down the hallway came a shout, "Patient in 266 in V-tach!" That's ventricular tachycardia, an irregular and furious pounding of the heart—in Darrell's case, a malignant 220 beats per minute. V-tach frequently appears at the beginning of a cardiac arrest—the point at which all beating stops and the jagged line on the heart monitor falls flat.

There's sometimes a gap of several seconds between when the arrest begins and the patient realizes something's wrong. As the hospital staff come running with a crash cart, the patient's last, frantic words before passing out might be, "You got the wrong guy!"

For Darrell, the gap was long enough for him to ask what was going on.

"Don't worry about it," the nurse replied. "You just need to relax."

Darrell was about to meet Jesus. *EEG available?*

At least that's how he would later identify the spirit being he saw.

It was Sunday morning, 9:50 A.M., July 31, 1994. The central heart monitor at the nurse's station was setting off an alarm that filled the entire cardiac unit with the high-pitched and rapid DING, DING, DING indicating a heart in V-tach. Nurses and doctors ran to Darrell's room.

"My forehead was sweaty and I was cold and shivery," Darrell told me. "A gentleman on my left-hand side took off my glasses and told me to cough a couple of times." A cough temporarily slows down the heart, much like a sneeze forces the eyelids shut in reflex. Sometimes this can convert the heart back to a normal rhythm.

It didn't work for Darrell.

"A guy threw a mask over my face and told me to breathe deeply," Darrell said. "I began to get faint. I breathed three times. Boom. I was out. I could hear at first, but then the voices were getting fainter."

Though no longer a practicing Christian, Darrell began to recite Bible verses he recalled from childhood. John 3:16, "For God so loved the world, that he gave his only begotten Son, that whosoever believeth in him should not perish, but have everlasting life." Psalm 23, "The Lord is my shepherd; I shall not want. . . ."

Suddenly, everything around Darrell became sky blue—he was completely engulfed in it. "I looked at this real pretty blue and then I saw the faces of all my friends and loved ones: my daughter, my wife, her mother and dad, my mom and dad." The pictures raced by like a high-speed, panoramic slide show.

All the while, Darrell continued to recite the psalm, until he finished the fourth verse: "Yea, though I walk through the valley of the shadow of death, I will fear no evil: for thou art with me; thy rod and thy staff they comfort me." The faces stopped, and Darrell found himself hovering at ceiling level, looking down on a team of six doctors and nurses working on his body.

Darrell wasn't watching alone.

At his right side stood "the Lord Jesus Christ," Darrell said, "with his left arm wrapped around me." Reddish-brown hair hung shoulder length on the spirit being, draping around the back of the spirit's blue T-shirt.

"I kept thinking, 'I can't die, Lord, because I've got my little girl and I've got my wife.'"

The only response of the spirit being was silence, and the hand that continued to rest on Darrell's shoulder.

A few feet below, the medical team shocked Darrell's body with 360 joules, or watt-seconds, converting his heart to atrial flutter, a slower, more stable rhythm of about 160 beats per minute. Ten minutes later they hit him again, this time with 50 joules followed by 200 joules in an unsuccessful effort to further slow his heart to normal rhythm. After 10 more minutes they tried a third time, again without success.

Darrell had been admitted to the hospital not only to await a transplant, but first to stabilize his rapidly failing heart. For some unknown reason, his heart muscle was becoming increasingly flaccid and limp. With each squeeze, a healthy heart ejects 60% of the blood inside the left ventricle; Darrell's was ejecting only 9%. The rest was backing up into his lungs instead of being distributed throughout his body. For almost a year, medication had assisted his heart. But now the medication was no longer working, and doctors were afraid they had missed the window of opportunity for a transplant.

Rushing to Save Darrell

In a dramatic effort to save Darrell, the cardiologist in charge decided to cut open Darrell's right femoral artery near the groin, insert a sausage-shaped balloon pump, and thread it through the artery and up beside the heart. Once in place, the pump is synchronized to inflate and deflate with the rhythm of the heart. During deflation, the balloon helps draw blood out of the failing heart. Inflation helps push blood into the network of arteries and veins throughout the body.

"I saw what they were doing," Darrell said, "but I didn't know what they were talking about. It was just gibberish. It sounded like confusion in there."

In fact, such an emergency procedure done in the patient's room is like a Chinese fire drill.

"It was not a real smooth balloon insertion," said Sandy Sherman, the weekend nurse on hand. "Getting all the stuff there, and trying to get all the equipment."

As Darrell hovered near the ceiling, he saw Sandy wearing her pink uniform and standing at his right side, near his head. The cardiologist and two other men were clustered around his right leg, two wearing green scrubs and one wearing blue. A male nurse in blue scrubs stood at the foot of the bed on the left side.

Suddenly Darrell woke up in his body. "I looked straight up and saw Sandy there." She was dressed in pink. He scanned the room and saw the others, confirming for himself what he had seen from outside of his body.

Darrell's wife, Alison, said that the first words he spoke to her after this were, "Don't worry about me. It's not so bad over there. It's really not."

The hospital code report shows that Darrell suffered four more arrests that day: at 1:10 P.M., 1:37 P.M., 6:50 P.M., and 7:10 P.M. Darrell also told me of having two more nearly identical out-of-body experiences. During each, he quoted the same Bible verses, saw the same faces racing by, and, with his spirit companion, watched the hospital staff work on his body. The staff confirms that he recited Scripture: "He would start quoting it when he felt himself getting dizzy," said one of his nurses. "When he came to he would still be quoting it, but he would be later on in the psalm. So he must have been quoting it while he was out."

"The third experience was the best," Darrell said. Only then did the spirit being speak, and only a single word, not from voice box to eardrum, but in the inaudible language of spirit to spirit.

The word, Darrell believes, related to concerns he felt as he watched the doctors resuscitating him. Though Darrell had told his wife not to worry about him, he was worried about her; they had been married for only five weeks. He was worried, too, about his eight-year-old daughter from a previous marriage; she wasn't getting along with her stepfather.

"I asked the Lord, 'What do you want me to do?' and he just said, 'Go.' *Bam!* I felt the [electric] shock that time. I came right back to earth that quick."

On the basis of that one word, "Go," Darrell returned with a deep assurance that he was going to live, receive the transplant, and be there for his family.

The Light that Came into the Room

Around 11 P.M. that night, friends who had comforted Alison throughout the day went home to their families. Alison sat alone at her husband's bedside, cradling his hand in hers and weeping quietly. She had been raised in a Southern Baptist home. Her dad was an ordained minister. Though she had stopped attending church during her late teens, she still remembered how to pray. While sitting at the bedside, she confessed her sins and promised to live a more godly life.

"I guess I felt that I had to get rid of all that stuff before I could start asking for favors," she said. "That's when I started asking for healing for Darrell, and that's when I opened my eyes."

What she saw would have terrified others, but it filled Alison with the joy that springs from heavenly assurance that Darrell would recover.

"There was light all around him," Alison said. "Around his head and shoulders, and real deep over his heart. It was so pretty. White and gold."

The light had framed Darrell's upper body, and a foot-long beam hovered like a pillar above his heart. Inside the light, streams of gold and white flowed gently, like waves inside a lava lamp.

In wonderment, Alison stared for several long moments before closing her eyes and whispering, "Thank you." She said that for at least an hour her eyes remained closed as she thanked God for what she had seen.

Then she asked for more.

"I said 'Lord, I'm going to open my eyes again. Put your hand on his heart, and put your other hand on our hands and show me that this is real.' And when I opened my eyes, there was this person on [Darrell's] left side."

The right hand of this spirit being rested on Darrell's heart, and his left hand held the clasped hands of Alison and Darrell.

"That's when I really, really knew Darrell was going to be okay."

Alison said the spirit being was Jesus. He knelt on the bed, eyes fixed on Darrell.

"He was not big," Alison said. He wore a white robe with a blue sash. His hair hung long and brown. Alison said she felt his hand. "It was cool. Not cold. Not especially warm. Like if you put your hand on my hand right now."

She said he was made of light, yet not transparent.

"I closed my eyes and started giving thanks again. Darrell woke up a little later and I said, 'Did you know that Jesus was here?' He said, 'Yeah.' And I said, 'Where was he?' and he patted the bed right there where [Jesus] was."

Within an hour or two, at 2:27 A.M., Darrell suffered the sixth of what would become 10 arrests spanning four days.

A Changed Woman

When I interviewed the nursing staff nine months later, they remembered Alison. But they described two different people. The Alison of Sunday was frantic, distraught, and combative. During efforts to resuscitate Darrell, she sequestered herself in the Gardenia Room, a private waiting area in which, at times, she would not even allow family and friends who had come to comfort her. Weekend nurse Sandy Sherman went to Alison that evening and asked if they could talk.

"She put her hand up and wouldn't look at me," Sandy recalled. "She said, 'I can't take this right now! I don't want anything to do with it right now!' I backed off and said, 'I'm not trying to push on you. It's okay.' The encounter was definitely not friendly."

But by Monday, even as the attacks persisted, Alison's anxiety had abated—an effect she attributes to her late-night meeting with the being of light. "She was very calm," said Louise Levy, a weekday nurse who began her 12-hour shift Monday morning. "When Darrell would arrest, she'd just quietly get up and leave the room. She didn't get upset. You know, a lot of family members freak out, pass out, become hysterical. She was very, very serene."

Tuesday, the cardiac arrests continued to break through all attempts to block them. And each shock that resuscitated Darrell further weakened his heart muscle. The cardiologist became convinced that Darrell would not survive resuscitation efforts much longer. And even if a donor heart became available, Darrell's condition was too unstable for surgery.

At four o'clock that morning Alison went home—for the first time since Sunday. But by 9:30 A.M. the hospital was on the phone urging her to come back right away. Darrell had suffered his eighth arrest. In the tiny Gardenia Room, Alison met with the cardiologist and three of his colleagues, including hospital transplant coordinator Patricia Aldridge, a registered nurse.

"The doctor talked with me about the fact that I needed to make a decision to discontinue [Darrell's] medications and let him die," Alison recalled. "He said, 'You know, he's not going to get any better. We've not been able to stabilize him. If we don't stabilize him here, we're going to pull him off the transplant list.'"

Transplant coordinator Patricia Aldridge, also a bride of just a few weeks, began to cry.

"No," Alison replied. "He's going to be fine."

Patricia vividly remembers that meeting. "We were all concerned that there was an element of denial here, that she was not facing reality," Patricia said. "But she stood very strong and very determined in her belief."

The doctor said he'd let Alison think about it. Then he and the two men with him left. Patricia and Alison remained.

"My voice was quivering," Patricia said. "I had tears in my eyes, streaming down my face. I had Kleenex in my hand, wiping my eyes." With a voice that kept breaking words into pieces and making Patricia feel less than professional, she asked a barrage of questions: "How was she so sure? Why was she so strong? And why did she believe so much that this was going to work out?"

Alison said only that she had faith. The women embraced. "It was Alison's husband who was dying," Patricia said, "and she had to comfort me."

Patricia and Alison cleaned up their faces and walked down the hall to Darrell's room.

Darrell knew the doctor had met with Alison, and he asked why.

Alison told him. She said the doctor wanted her to decide if they should stop the medication and resuscitation efforts. Then she said, "Here's how I feel about it. I feel like I've had assurance that you're going to be fine. But it's your decision too."

Darrell replied, "No. I don't want to die. I want to live. Don't do it."

Alison assured him, "Okay, I won't."

They made the right decision. Two weeks later a team of surgeons and medical staff gave Darrell the new heart he needed. Within weeks, his recovery was complete. But the effect this experience had on him was just beginning.

A Changed Man

Alison was not the only person profoundly changed by the events of that dramatic Sunday just weeks before. Darrell changed even more markedly.

Though he also had been raised a Southern Baptist, he too withdrew from church and religion as a teenager, when his church had revoked the membership of his alcoholic father. Darrell himself became an alcoholic as well as a drug user. He was arrested three times for driving under the influence of alcohol. Five times he had been put in jail. This alcohol and drug abuse, along with the run-ins with the law, wreaked havoc with his personal life. His first two marriages ended in divorce, and on his first date with Alison he got horribly drunk. Though Darrell started going to Alcoholics Anonymous and hadn't had a drink for almost two years (the transplant program required him to abstain), religion wasn't on his agenda.

Louise Levy, one of Darrell's primary nurses, described the change that took place in him after Sunday, July 31. "He never mentioned religion before, and he talked about little else after."

Weekend nurse Sandy Sherman said that before Sunday, "His eyes had no life in them. He looked sad and scared." But by the following Saturday, after suffering 10 arrests, "There was a light in his eyes. There was a joy there."

She said her first clue came that same Saturday morning when she was in a patient's room on the other side of the unit, some 20 yards away. "I could hear someone singing at the top of their lungs, 'How Great Thou Art.'"

It was Darrell.

A few days later, when Darrell asked to read anything in the hospital about out-of-body experiences, the nurse on duty insisted that the librarian bring it up personally.

"I argued that I don't see patients," said librarian Joan Drummond, "but the nurse argued that I *had* to see this one. I fussed all the way up there about having to go."

She said it was worth the fuss.

"He had the most intense eyes I had ever seen outside of my mother's when she was dying. It was like he was looking into my soul to make sure it was okay to talk to me."

But they did talk. Though Darrell was weak, for the next 20 minutes he told her about his experience, and why he no longer feared death. "I came out of there so emotionally drenched because I felt he was in the presence of God," Joan said. "I was crying when I came out."

The Morning I Met Darrell

I met and first interviewed Darrell on the Saturday morning he serenaded the cardiac unit with hymns, six days after his out-of-body experiences. While I was making rounds, a nurse who knew of my interest in the subject told me I should see the patient who had "come real close to God." After I got permission from Darrell's physician, I walked into his room. He was lying in bed reading a Bible, the television humming in the background.

The man I saw was short and stocky; his medical chart listed him as five-foot-seven and 143 pounds. His skin was bronzed and his cheekbones high, features inherited perhaps from Mexican or Native American ancestors (adopted as an infant, Darrell doesn't know who his birth parents are). His black hair lay in foot-long strands, thick and wavy on the pillow. A mustache and beard framed his mouth and chin and crept partway up his cheeks.

I introduced myself and said I was interested in talking with people who had come close to death. He propped himself up higher in bed, turned off the TV and eagerly began to tell me about what he called "the best week of my whole life."

When I stopped by to visit him the next day, he showed me a picture he had just drawn of his near-death experience. The crayon-colored scene showed Darrell and someone else looking down on his body, which was lying on the bed surrounded by hospital staff. He had tacked the picture to the wall at the foot of his bed as a perpetual reminder of his encounter with Jesus.

It didn't dawn on me until nine months later, after I revisited the room, that the drawing put Darrell and Jesus above the doorway. There, as in each patient's room, hangs a gold-colored cruci-fix of Jesus.

Coincidence? Perhaps. But a crop of goose bumps exploded on my back nonetheless.

Changed for the Long Haul

Whatever it was that Darrell saw during his NDE, he was changed radically for the long haul. Almost a year later I talked with Louise Levy, who still sees Darrell when he comes in for routine heart biopsies. She said, "Most people calm down after a while, if you know what I mean. He hasn't really done that. He still wears his button that says 'Jesus.' And he talks about how God has blessed him in tiny little ways in his life every time I see him, which is often."

He does this at the grocery store too, says his wife. And frankly, it gets on her nerves. "We will be standing in line," says Alison, "and suddenly he'll just find any excuse to say, 'Look, I just had a heart transplant and the Lord changed my life.' He preaches all the time. Finally I had to sit him down and say, 'Don't you have another topic of conversation?'"

Alison is a churchgoing bartender who feels that she provides a positive example to the customers. Darrell says he wants her out of there soon. But in the meantime, he visits her at work—wearing a leather motorcycle vest that's a virtual quilt of religious patches: "Riding for the Son," "Christian Motorcyclists Association," "Prayer Team," "100% for Jesus," "Jesus #1." He wears these, he said, because he may be the last Bible some people ever see.

The Darrell that Alison met and married is not the Darrell she lives with now. "He is a totally different person," she says, and getting used to him "has been very difficult."

Darrell is also a different man than transplant coordinator Patricia Aldridge came to know during her many meetings with him throughout the year before his surgery. Transplant patients reveal a lot about themselves during these sessions. "They become a second family to us, and us to them," Patricia said. "We know these people for the rest of their lives." She said Darrell never mentioned religion before the series of cardiac arrests. But now, she says, he regularly visits the hospital, seeing patients, sharing his experience with them, praying, and reading Scripture.

This isn't the only volunteer ministry Darrell launched after his near-death experience. He also regularly visits Atlanta area prisons, counsels juvenile delinquents, and talks about Jesus to bikers who attend motorcycle rallies.

"I don't know why the Lord wanted me to work in this ministry," Darrell says. But through an unspoken, inner voice, "the Lord just told me 'motorcycles, prisons, and children.'"

Darrell didn't even have a motorcycle at the time. But a week after he got out of the hospital, he noticed a church sign along the road that said the Christian Motorcyclists Association would be holding a service in a few weeks. Darrell was there.

After the service, he stumbled over to the state coordinator and asked, "What does it take to be in this organization?"

He responded, "Are you a Christian?"

Darrell said, "Yeah."

"Praise the Lord, you're admitted."

When the coordinator asked what Darrell was riding, Darrell responded, "A car."

Yet even without a motorcycle, a month later his local chapter asked him to serve as road captain—the person responsible for plotting the routes to motorcycle rallies throughout the region. He agreed, then bought himself a 10-year-old Harley Davidson Superglide.

"I didn't like it," Darrell said. "The seat was torn, there were scratches in the saddlebag, there were scratches on the windshield. Then I thought, *Well, you know what, I was scratched and damaged like that too, but the Lord accepted me.*"

He bought the bike with the help of collateral put up by Alison's dad. He christened it Second Chance, and had the name painted in brilliant white cursive, outlined in blood red, on the top left side of the gas tank. On the right side is a Valentine's heart, cracked and broken open in the center. Butterflies are fluttering out of its ragged tear, a symbol of Darrell's new life.

Darrell and Alison joined a church on the first Easter Sunday after the transplant. On the day that Christians commemorate the resurrection of Jesus, Darrell memorialized his own rebirth— a physical and spiritual rebirth that began in room 266 of Saint Joseph's cardiac unit as he and a spirit being he calls Jesus watched doctors retrieve him from the brink of death.

Revisiting Darrell's Interview

I couldn't believe that when I first met Darrell in the coronary care unit that Saturday morning he claimed to have just had the "best week" of his life. Yet he went on to describe 10 cardiac arrests, multiple painful medical procedures, and a near decision to discontinue treatment and to let him die. *This was Darrell's idea of a "best week,"* I wondered? It didn't add up.

So I thumbed through his medical chart looking for clues. One nursing entry three days after Darrell's first arrest caught my eye: "Patient has strong Christian faith and he says this has carried him throughout these tough times."

In exploring this further, Darrell recalled a faith that initially had been weak. But following the first NDE, he explained, his faith radically strengthened and was now sustaining him like never before. Alison, too, had intensely prayed for his healing and had been assured of his survival by a spiritual light she called Jesus.

During my first interview, both Darrell and Alison were absolutely convinced that Darrell would receive a heart transplant and live, even though, at the time, this outcome was still medically in doubt. I couldn't help but wonder whether the powerful spiritual events surrounding Darrell's near-death experiences had somehow determined his final medical outcome.

Other questions swirled through my mind as I sat listening to his story. How close to death had Darrell actually come? If Darrell had not been a Christian, would his NDE have been different, as some claim?

The Atlanta Study

Because of questions such as these raised by patients like Darrell and because of my increasing unrest with discussions of the NDE in the media, in 1994 I launched The Atlanta Study. Armed again with a tape recorder and carefully constructed, measurable questionnaires, I started what became two years of interviewing 160 patients, most of whom were from my own clinical practice. Forty-seven of these had NDEs; the rest of the group were used to create a baseline comparison. I called this project The Atlanta Study, since that's where I practice medicine, and where many of the study subjects live.

In this study, I wanted to explore the relationship between faith, medicine, and the near-death experience. And I wanted to do it like it had never been done before.

First, I would ensure that each person entered in my study had survived a clearly defined near-death experience associated with a near-fatal physical crisis and unconsciousness. The experience would need to meet the research criteria established by Dr. Bruce Greyson for a near-death experience.[1] Greyson had devised an NDE Scale, which allowed for quantification of the depth of an experience based on graded responses to 16 questions. Scores ranged from 0 to 32. The higher the score, the deeper the experience. A minimum score of 7 was needed to qualify as a near-death experience.

Next, I would pursue virgin cases of the near-death experience. I would interview only people who had not told their story to a mass audience. People who told their stories widely, I feared, could easily begin to confuse fact with fiction as they tried to hold the attention of a restless audience. I also would *not* use the standard research pool from which most case studies are drawn: the International Association for Near-Death Studies (IANDS). My feeling was, and is, that many IANDS members are like-minded people who have communicated with one another, subscribe to the association journal, go to the annual conferences, participate in local support groups, and read books by IANDS researchers, which is the vast majority of the near-death literature. Evaluating the religious beliefs of these people, I felt, would likely produce slanted results.

I also wanted to clearly differentiate between types of religious believers. Since 87% of the American population is Christian, my study groups would be divided most logically into Christians, believers in God who are not Christians (I refer to these as "God-believers"), and atheists. I was also curious about whether there was any difference between Christians who hold traditional, conservative religious beliefs and Christians who are more liberal-minded and ecumenical. Most researchers tend to lump all self-proclaimed Christians together. The problem with this approach is that some who claim to be Christian or indicate "Christian" on a survey actually believe the traditional doctrine that Jesus was the divine son of God, while others mean they are Christian in a more general or cultural sense but do not hold to such a strict doctrinal position. I created a Spiritual Beliefs Questionnaire to distinguish between traditional Christians, liberal Christians, God-believers, and atheists.

During two years of searching, I found 28 women and 19 men who had had a near-death experience. Their ages ranged from 33 to 82 years, and they were from many walks of life: teacher, housewife, architect, physician, truck driver, lumberman, insurance agent, musician, engineer, and secretary, to name a few.

In the group were 22 traditional Christians, 13 liberal Christians, 12 God-believers, and no atheists (see Table 1 in Appendix).

Nine people reported more than one NDE. In these cases, the person's deepest near-death experience was used as the "index" NDE for statistical comparisons within the overall group. These 47 statistically-compared NDEs were associated collectively with 23 cardiac arrests; 14 episodes of shock (mainly hemorrhagic); 4 accidents (3 auto, 1 war); 4 overdoses (2 intentional, 2 unintentional); 1 bout of respiratory failure; and 1 surgical procedure during which all vital signs were lost (see Table 5 in Appendix).

I examined each person's medical records when available and queried them about their private and family life, church involvement, and other spiritual activities. I used surveys to measure their inner spirituality. I also asked a barrage of questions designed by other NDE researchers so I could compare my findings with those of previous studies.

To help measure the accuracy of the results, I added two control groups from my medical practice who did not have a near-death experience: (1) a group of 81 who responded to surveys I mailed to 100 consecutive patients; and (2) 32 people who had open-heart surgery. These control groups would help me sort out the side effects unique to the near-death experience, as opposed to effects common among people whether or not they've faced death, and common among those who have a brush with death but without a near-death experience.

Seventy percent of the 160 total participants in The Atlanta Study turned out to be Protestant, 14% Catholic, 6% Jewish, 4% from other faiths, and 5% with no formal affiliation. One person was an atheist. These percentages align very closely with numbers derived from national polls of people's beliefs in America.

What I found when I tallied the data surprised me. Exciting new evidence suggested a definite link between faith, survival, and the near-death experience. In addition, I discovered that a near-death experience affected one's religious faith and practice differently from what I was hearing in the media.

One of the most disorienting surprises, however, involved medicine and the definition of death. Prior to The Atlanta Study, I had been confident that NDEs were *near-death experiences*, not *after-death* experiences, and that the line between life and death was clearly defined. Then I met Pam Reynolds, the person who had the deepest near-death experience in The Atlanta Study.

By every method that scientists use to measure life, she was flatlined—no blood pressure, breathing, heartbeat, or brain waves. Even the blood had been drained from her head.

So uncertain is men's judgment that they cannot determine even death itself.[1]

—PLINY THE ELDER
HISTORIA NATURALIS, A. D. 77

Three

DEATH:

Defining the Final Frontier

The Midas Rex whirlwind bone saw, rotating at a constant 73,000 rpm, was deftly held by the surgeon like a brush in the hand of an artist. A loud whirring noise, similar to that of a dentist's drill, filled the sterile air of the operating room.[2]

Brain surgery was about to begin.

Thirty-five-year-old Pam Reynolds was being operated on for a giant basilar artery aneurysm. A weakness in the wall of the large artery at the base of her brain had caused it to balloon out much like a bubble on the side of a defective automobile tire. Rupture of the aneurysm would be immediately fatal.

The size and location of the aneurysm, however, precluded its safe removal using the standard neurosurgical techniques available to Pam in her hometown of Atlanta. She had been referred to Dr. Robert Spetzler, Director of Barrow Neurological Institute in Phoenix, Arizona. Spetzler had pioneered a daring surgical procedure known as hypothermic cardiac arrest, which would allow Pam's aneurysm to be excised with a reasonable chance of success. This operation, nicknamed "standstill" by the doctors who perform it, would require that her body temperature be lowered to 60 degrees, her heartbeat and breathing stopped, her brain waves flattened, and the blood drained from her head. In everyday terms she would be dead. But in the hands of skilled physicians she was not. Or was she?

The question of when death occurs is raised frequently in discussions of the near-death experience. To understand scientifically the relationship of death to the near-death experience, we must first measure as precisely as possible the physiologic state of the body during the NDE. Unfortunately, most popular NDE accounts come with little or no verification of the purported medical crisis or of physiologic parameters such as brain-wave activity, blood pressure, cardiac rhythm, et cetera. The whole episode frequently rests on self-report alone. In The Atlanta Study, however, medical documentation of the events surrounding the near-death experience was obtained whenever possible. In Pam's case, this documentation *far exceeds* any recorded before and provides us with our most complete scientific glimpse yet into the near-death experience.

Pam had been awake when brought into the operating room at 7:15 that August morning in 1991. She remembers the IVs, "so many of them," followed by "a loss of time" as the intravenous penthathol worked its calming magic on her.

According to Spetzler's surgical report, her body was lifted onto the operating table and her arms and legs securely tied down. Her eyes were lubricated to prevent drying and then taped shut. An endotracheal tube was skillfully guided through her mouth into her windpipe, and general anesthesia was begun.

For the next hour and twenty-five minutes, Pam's unconscious body was instrumented with the most advanced technology, some of which had been specifically designed for hypothermic arrest.

A two-inch-long plastic tube was slipped into the artery in her wrist to continuously monitor her blood pressure. A three-foot long Swan Ganz catheter, resembling an elongated piece of spaghetti, was threaded through the jugular vein of her neck into the artery in her lung to measure pulmonary pressures and blood flow from her heart. Cardiac monitoring leads were attached to follow heart rate and rhythm, and an oximeter was taped to her index finger to measure oxygen levels in her blood.

Precise documentation of body temperature would be crucial. Urinary temperature would be measured by a special thermister on the tip of a Foley catheter placed in Pam's bladder.

o

Core body temperature from the innermost part of her body would be monitored with another thermistor placed deeply into her esophagus. The temperature of her brain would be registered through a thin wire embedded in its surface.

Standard EEG electrodes taped to her head would record cerebral cortical brain activity. The auditory nerve center located in the brain stem would be tested repeatedly using 100-decibel clicks emitted from small, molded speakers inserted into her ears. In response to these clicks, sharp spikes on the electrogram (i.e., evoked potentials) would assure the surgical team that the brain stem was intact.

Four separate sites were prepped for surgery: the right side of Pam's head for the craniotomy, the chest for possible open-heart surgery, and both groins for femoral artery and vein access for cardiopulmonary bypass. Adhesive defibrillator pads were stuck to her chest in case her heart needed to be shocked back to life.

Finally, Pam's head was turned to a full left lateral position and secured in a three-point-pin head holder.

By 8:40 A.M., Pam's entire body except for her head and groin had been blanketed with sterile drapes. Over 20 doctors, nurses, and technicians had scrubbed in (see Figure 1).

Surrounding Pam's head was the neurosurgical team, including Spetzler, who sat in a specialized chair controlled by foot pedals, leaving both hands free to operate. To the right of her legs stood the cardiac surgical team. At her feet sat the heart–pump technicians with their giant chrome-headed pump oxygenator and cardiopulmonary bypass equipment. And to her left were the neuroanesthesiologists, who were monitoring her vital signs and brain function. Perfect coordination among these four medical teams would be critical if the aneurysm were to be successfully removed and Pam retrieved from her journey to the edge of death.

Spetzler began the surgery by carefully marking the incision lines on Pam's shaved head and quickly opening the scalp with a

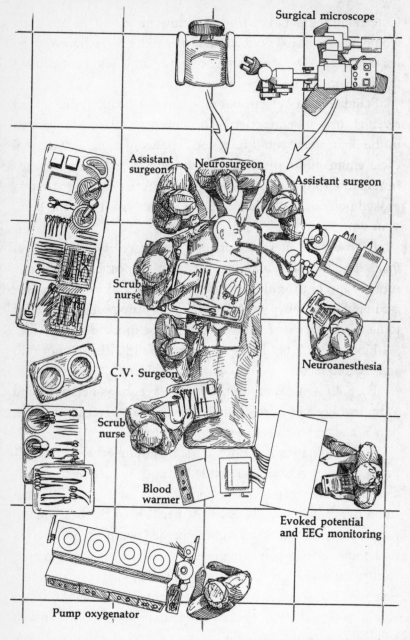

Figure 1: Diagram of the operating room at Barrow Neurological Institute from a perspective similar to Pam's out-of-body experience. Illustration courtesy of Barrow Neurological Institute.

curved surgical blade. The scalp flap was folded back, exposing a glistening gray skull. A surgical nurse handed Spetzler the pneumatically-powered Midas Rex, attached by a long green hose to compressed air tanks in the corner of the room. A loud buzzing noise then filled the OR as the powerful, thumb-sized motor hidden in the brass head of the bone saw revved up. The cutting tool began to carve out a large section of Pam's skull.

Pam's near-death experience began to unfold. She relates the story with remarkable detail:

> The next thing I recall was the sound: It was a natural *D*. As I listened to the sound, I felt it was pulling me out of the top of my head. The further out of my body I got, the more clear the tone became. I had the impression it was like a road, a frequency that you go on.... I remember seeing several things in the operating room when I was looking down. It was the most aware that I think that I have ever been in my entire life.... I was metaphorically sitting on Dr. Spetzler's shoulder. It was not like normal vision. It was brighter and more focused and clearer than normal vision.... There was so much in the operating room that I didn't recognize, and so many people.
>
> I thought the way they had my head shaved was very peculiar. I expected them to take all of the hair, but they did not....
>
> The saw thing that I hated the sound of looked like an electric toothbrush and it had a dent in it, a groove at the top where the saw appeared to go into the handle, but it didn't.... And the saw had interchangeable blades, too, but these blades were in what looked like a socket wrench case.... I heard the saw crank up. I didn't see them use it on my head, but I think I heard it being used on something. It was humming at a relatively high pitch and then all of a sudden it went *Brrrrrrrrr!* like that.

Spetzler removed the bone flap from Pam's skull, exposing the outermost membrane of her brain—the dura mater. This tough, fibrous covering was opened with special dural scissors. The operating microscope was then draped and swung into position. The remainder of the intracranial portion of the procedure took place under this microscope controlled by a lever held in Spetzler's mouth.

While Spetzler was opening Pam's head, a female cardiac surgeon located the femoral artery and vein in Pam's right groin. These vessels turned out to be too small to handle the large flow of blood needed to feed the cardiopulmonary bypass machine. Thus, the left femoral artery and vein were prepared for use. Pam later recalled this point in the surgery:

> Someone said something about my veins and arteries being very small. I believe it was a female voice and that it was Dr. Murray, but I'm not sure. She was the cardiologist [*sic*]. I remember thinking that I should have told her about that . . . . I remember the heart-lung machine. I didn't like the respirator. . . . I remember a lot of tools and instruments that I did not readily recognize.

Attention then shifted to large color television monitors mounted on the OR walls, which began to televise Pam's brain as seen through the operating microscope. The OR team followed Spetzler on the TV screen as he journeyed underneath the base of the temporal lobe, around the vein of Labbe, between the third and fourth cranial nerves, and to the neck of a giant basilar artery aneurysm. As feared, the aneurysm turned out to be, as Spetzler noted in his medical records, "extremely large and extended up into the brain." Hypothermic cardiac arrest would definitely be needed.

Into the Valley of the Shadow of Death

At 10:50 A.M. the cardiac surgeon and heart-pump technicians leapt into action. Tubes were inserted into the exposed femoral arteries and veins and connected to clear plastic hoses leading to and from the cardiopulmonary bypass machine. Warm blood from Pam's body began coursing through the hoses into the large reservoir cylinders of the bypass machine. Here it would be chilled before being returned to her body. The risky cooling process had begun.

At 11:00 A.M. Pam's core body temperature had fallen 25 degrees. The methodical beep-beep-beep of the cardiac monitor was interrupted by a steady warning tone indicating cardiac malfunction. The irregular, disorganized pattern of ventricular fibrillation now marched across the monitor screen. Five minutes later, the remaining electrical spasms of Pam's dying heart were extinguished with massive intravenous doses of potassium chloride. Cardiac arrest was complete.   *esp̌t.*   ?

As Pam's heart arrested, her brain waves flattened into complete electrocerebral silence. Brain-stem function weakened as the clicks from the ear speakers produced lower and lower spikes on the monitoring electrogram.

Twenty minutes later, her core body temperature had fallen another 13 degrees to a tomblike 60 degrees Fahrenheit. The clicks from her ear speakers no longer elicited a response. Total brain shutdown.

Then, at precisely 11:25 A.M., Pam was subjected to one of the most daring and remarkable surgical maneuvers ever performed in an operating room. The head of the operating table was tilted up, the cardiopulmonary bypass machine was turned off, and the blood was drained from Pam's body like oil from a car. Sometime during this period, Pam's near-death experience progressed:

> There was a sensation like being pulled, but not against your will. I was going on my own accord because I wanted to go. I have different metaphors to try to explain this. It was like the Wizard of Oz—being taken up in a tornado vortex, only you're

not spinning around like you've got vertigo. You're very focused and you have a place to go. The feeling was like going up in an elevator real fast. And there was a sensation, but it wasn't a bodily, physical sensation. It was like a tunnel but it wasn't a tunnel.

At some point very early in the tunnel vortex I became aware of my grandmother calling me. But I didn't hear her call me with my ears. . . . It was a clearer hearing than with my ears. I trust that sense more than I trust my own ears. The feeling was that she wanted me to come to her, so I continued with no fear down the shaft. It's a dark shaft that I went through, and at the very end there was this very little tiny pinpoint of light that kept getting bigger and bigger and bigger.

The light was incredibly bright, like sitting in the middle of a lightbulb. It was so bright that I put my hands in front of my face fully expecting to see them and I could not. But I knew they were there. Not from a sense of touch. Again, it's terribly hard to explain, but I knew they were there. . . .

I noticed that as I began to discern different figures in the light—and they were all covered with light, they *were* light, and had light permeating all around them—they began to form shapes I could recognize and understand. I could see that one of them was my grandmother. I don't know if it was reality or projection, but I would know my grandmother, the sound of her, anytime, anywhere.

Everyone I saw, looking back on it, fit perfectly into my understanding of what that person looked like at their best during their lives.

I recognized a lot of people. My uncle Gene was there. So was my great-great-Aunt Maggie, who was really a cousin. On Papa's side of the family, my grandfather was there. . . . They were specifically taking care of me, looking after me.

They would not permit me to go further. . . . It was communicated to me—that's the best way I know how to say it, because they didn't speak like I'm speaking—that if I went all the way into the light something would happen to me physically. They would be unable to put this me back into the body me, like I had gone too far and they couldn't reconnect. So they wouldn't let me go anywhere or do anything.

I wanted to go into the light, but I also wanted to come back. I had children to be reared. It was like watching a movie on fast-forward on your VCR: You get the general idea, but the individual freeze-frames are not slow enough to get detail.

With the blood drained from her body, the aneurysm sac collapsed like a deflated balloon. Spetzler clipped the neck of the aneurysm at its point of attachment to the basilar artery and excised the empty sac. The cardiopulmonary bypass machine was then turned back on and warmed blood began to be reinfused into Pam's empty body.

Shortly after the warming had begun, the clicks from the speakers in Pam's ears registered the first signs of life with telltale blips on the electrogram. Reassuring waves of electrical activity from her higher brain centers began again to advance across the EEG screen. Pam's body appeared to be waking up, perhaps at a time during her near-death experience when she was being strengthened:

> Then they [deceased relatives] were feeding me. They were not doing this through my mouth, like with food, but they were nourishing me with something. The only way I know how to put it is something sparkly. Sparkles is the image that I get. I definitely recall the sensation of being nurtured and being fed and being made strong. I know it sounds funny, because obviously it wasn't a physical thing, but inside the experience I felt physically strong, ready for whatever.

Then, at 12:00 noon, a serious problem arose. The initially silent heart monitor began to register the disorganized electrical activity of ventricular fibrillation. Efforts to correct this lethal cardiac rhythm with additional warming were unsuccessful. If left uncorrected, Pam would die on the table within minutes.

The cardiac surgeon quickly placed the two defibrillator paddles on Pam's chest and shocked her heart with 50 joules of electricity. No response. The defibrillator was then charged with 100 joules and reapplied. After this second jolt of electricity, the familiar beep-beep-beep of normal sinus rhythm brought forth sighs of relief from the cardiac surgical team, who were preparing to cut open her chest to revive her heart.

And Pam began her "return" from her near-death experience:

> My grandmother didn't take me back through the tunnel, or even send me back or ask me to go. She just looked up at me. I expected to go with her, but it was communicated to me that she just didn't think she would do that. My uncle said he would do it. He's the one who took me back through the end of the tunnel. Everything was fine. I did want to go.
>
> But then I got to the end of it and saw the thing, my body. I didn't want to get into it. . . . It looked terrible, like a train wreck. It looked like what it was: dead. I believe it was covered. It scared me and I didn't want to look at it.
>
> It was communicated to me that it was like jumping into a swimming pool. No problem, just jump right into the swimming pool. I didn't want to, but I guess I was late or something because he [the uncle] pushed me. I felt a definite repelling and at the same time a pulling from the body. The body was pulling and the tunnel was pushing. . . . It was like diving into a pool of ice water. . . . It hurt!

With additional warming and reinfusion of blood, the cardiopulmonary bypass machine was turned off at 12:32 P.M., when Pam's temperature had reached a life-sustaining but still subnormal 89.6 degrees. Her body was then deinstrumented and her surgical wounds closed. The music in the background began playing rock as Spetzler's younger assistants took over the closing surgical duties. The songs did not escape Pam's notice:

> When I came back, they were playing "Hotel California" and the line was "You can check out anytime you like, but you can never leave." I mentioned [later] to Dr. Brown that that was incredibly insensitive and he told me that I needed to sleep more. [laughter] When I regained consciousness, I was still on the respirator.

Spetzler's surgical report indicates that at 2:10 P.M. the "patient was taken to the recovery room still intubated, but in stable condition."

Reconsidering Death and the "Near-Death" Experience

Ever since my earliest research into the near-death experience in the 1970s, I have consistently maintained that these are *near-death*, not *after*-death experiences. In *Recollections of Death*, I found that the closer one came to death, the more likely one would later report a near-death experience. That is, patients who had been hospitalized at the time of their near-death crisis events, who had been unconscious for longer periods of time, and who had required medical resuscitation for survival, were much more likely to report NDEs than those surviving out-of-hospital events associated with briefer periods of unconsciousness and unassisted resuscitation.

Being close to death, *no matter how close*, was still a far cry from being dead.

Then Pam's story jostled my certainty. When I first read her operative report at her mother's home in November 1994, I was incredulous. Who, in their right mind, would eliminate all of a person's vital signs, chill her body to 60 degrees, drain her blood, and still expect her to live? I *really* could not believe it! So I phoned the Barrow Neurological Institute and had them fax me *their* copy of Spetzler's report along with the operative summaries of the neuroanesthesiologist and cardiac surgeon.

Much to my surprise, I found the surgical details of Pam's story corroborated. Had her surgeons brought her back from the dead? Based on old definitions of death they had done just that.

The scientific definition of death is a medical quagmire. Previously, death was declared when a person was found unconscious without pulse or respiration. Death was confirmed by holding a mirror under the nose to test for condensation and by checking the pupils for a reaction to light. In the mid-nineteenth century, the invention of the stethoscope enabled doctors to diagnose death by the absence of heart sounds. The electrocardiogram made this diagnosis more secure by recording loss of electrical activity in the heart.

This so-called heart-lung criteria of death fell out of favor, however, with the advent of cardiopulmonary resuscitation (CPR), which enabled persons pronounced "dead"—without heartbeat and respiration—to be brought back to life. This necessitated a new definition of death: the loss of *brain* function. The brain is a complicated organ with markedly different divisions of structure and function: the cerebrum or "higher brain" controls consciousness, thought, feeling, and memory; the brain stem or "lower brain" controls the involuntary functions of respiration, yawning, and sleep-wake cycles; and the cerebellum controls balance and coordination. Initially, this diversity of brain function was not a problem in defining death since, according to the Uniform Determination of Death Act formulated by a special presidential commission in 1981, this diagnosis required the "cessation of all functions of the entire brain." This became known as the "whole brain" definition of death.

During CPR, however, the cerebrum was found to be more vulnerable to brief periods of absent blood flow and oxygen than was the brain stem. This set up the possibility that the "lower brain" could be saved after "higher brain" functions had been irreversibly lost—a condition known as the "persistent vegetative state." Such persons remain comatose, lose all awareness of self and environment, but maintain respiration and other "lower brain" functions. Loss of "higher brain" activity was then proposed as yet another definition of death to account for this situation which, to many, equalled death. Debate still rages, signaling the arbitrariness of deciding whether the "whole brain" or "higher brain" definition or neither of these two definitions of death is scientifically accurate.

Nonetheless, for practical purposes outside the world of academic debate, three clinical tests commonly determine brain death. First, a standard electroencephalogram, or EEG, measures brain-wave activity. A "flat" EEG denotes nonfunction of the cerebral cortex—the outer shell of the cerebrum. Second, auditory evoked potentials, similar to those elicited by the ear speakers in Pam's surgery, measure brain-stem viability. Absence of these potentials indicates nonfunction of the brain stem. And third, documentation of no blood flow to the brain is a marker for a generalized absence of brain function.

But during "standstill," Pam's brain was found "dead" by all three clinical tests—her electroencephalogram was silent, her brain-stem response was absent, and no blood flowed through her brain. Interestingly, while in this state, she encountered the "deepest" near-death experience of all Atlanta Study participants. The average score for an NDE on Dr. Greyson's NDE Scale was 15, similar to the 13.3 average I found in The Atlanta Study. Pam's NDE stood out, however, with an amazing depth of 27!

With this information, can we now scientifically assert that Pam was either dead or alive during her near-death experience? Unfortunately, no. Even if all medical tests certify her death, we would still have to wait to see if life was restored. Since she did

live, then *by definition* she was *never* dead. Doctors can save people
from death and rescue some who are close to death, but they cannot raise people from the dead. Conversely, if Pam had died, the
tests indicating death would have been confirmed.

On CBS' *48 Hours*, Dr. Spetzler was interviewed along with
Pam and myself. As Pam's attending surgeon, he emphasized that
during hypothermic cardiac arrest, "If you would examine that
patient from a clinical perspective during that hour, that patient
by all definition would be dead. At this point there is no brain
activity, no blood going through the brain. Nothing, nothing,
nothing."

When asked about Pam's near-death experience, the surgeon
delicately avoided the question: "One thing that I learned after
spending so many years of dealing with the brain is that nothing
is impossible."

Dr. Linda Emanuel, in the probing article "Reexamining
Death," writes:

> The reigning view [of death] has assumed that life and death
> are nonoverlapping, dichotomous states. This view acknowl-
> edges that dying may take time, but presumes that a threshold
> event is nevertheless definable; a person is thought to be either
> alive or dead, not both.... Is there an event that can identify
> final and complete loss of life? The answer appears to be no....
> The process of dying occurs at different levels of organization,
> from the organism to the organ, cellular, and subcellular levels,
> and each set of systems can decline on a somewhat indepen-
> dent trajectory.[3]

Several scientific observations support Emanuel's argument
that loss of biologic life, including death of the brain, is a process
and does not occur at a single, definite moment. Physicians at
Loyola University Medical Center found that 20% of patients had
persisting EEG activity up to seven days after extensive testing
had otherwise diagnosed brain death.[4] Normal function of the

pituitary gland (a part of the brain lying at the base of the skull) has been found several days after the diagnosis of brain death in patients.[5] And startling records of 10 organ donors diagnosed "brain-dead" showed an average increase in blood pressure of 31 millimeters of mercury and in heart rate of 23 beats per minute in response to surgical removal of the organs—reactions inconsistent with total cessation of brain function.[6] These findings indicate that even when a person is deemed "brain dead" by strict clinical criteria—that is, showing no spontaneous movements or respiration; no response to painful or auditory stimulation; and no brain stem, cough, gag, or respiratory reflexes—brain activity can often still be demonstrated days later, raising the question of *when*, if at all, death had actually occurred.

Thus, the problem with defining the moment of death lies not in our lack of sufficient scientific tools, but in the concept itself. There *is* no definable moment of death, but only a process of dying which starts with life and eventually ends in death. The journey through a near-death experience may best be understood as an experiential counterpart to this physical dying process. And whether this journey ends in life or in death is determined not only by the physical factors at play, but, as we shall see next, by events unseen by all except the unconscious, dying patient.

The practice of medicine ... is an art, based to an increasing extent on the medical sciences but comprising much that still remains outside the realm of any science.[1]

—FRANCIS W. PEABODY, M.D.
"THE CARE OF THE PATIENT"
THE JOURNAL OF THE
AMERICAN MEDICAL ASSOCIATION, 1927

SURVIVAL:

Behind the Scenes of a Cardiac Arrest

Since antiquity, people have been described as dying suddenly, while in the throes of extreme emotional upset. The notion of being "scared to death" or "frightened to death" is common in every culture. The Bible records the story of Ananias and his wife Sapphira (Acts 5:1–10). This couple sold a piece of land, retained a portion of the price for their personal use, and then brought the rest to the apostles for the benefit of the community.

When Ananias deceitfully represented the donated amount as the total received from the sale, the apostle Peter confronted him with the charge, "You have lied to the Holy Spirit."

Immediately, "he fell down and died."

Three hours later Sapphira arrived, unaware of her husband's fate. When Peter questioned her in a similar way, she repeated her husband's falsehood.

Peter responded, "The feet of the men who buried your husband are at the door, and they will carry you out also."

She, like Ananias, "fell down at his feet and died."

According to theologian Matthew Henry, Ananias' "own conscience smote him with such horror and amazement at the sense of his guilt, that he sunk and died away under the load of it." For Sapphira, "The sentence executed itself. There needed no executioner, a killing power went along with Peter's word, ... [and] struck her as a thunderbolt and took her away as with a whirlwind."[2]

Dr. George Engel, professor of medicine at the University of Rochester School of Medicine, studied the physiological mechanism responsible for sudden psychological death in 275 persons.[3]

He found that lethal emotional situations most commonly involve receiving news of the death of a loved one, loss of status or self-esteem, perception of personal danger, or threat of injury—all events eliciting overwhelming excitation and loss of control. Death in such situations, Dr. Engel postulated, results from a sharp rise in heart rate, blood pressure, and irregularities of heartbeat, which, in turn, lead to cardiac arrest.

In the predawn hours of January 17, 1994, one of the strongest earthquakes ever recorded in a major city in North America spread terror and fear throughout the streets of Los Angeles County. As predicted by Engel's hypothesis, persons on cardiac monitors registered an excessive number of dangerous rhythm disturbances from the emotional impact of the massive quake, and many in the population at large dropped dead.[4]

More recently, cardiac defibrillators—electroshock machines that can restart the heart by applying a shock to the chest—have been permanently installed at the New York Stock Exchange. Unpredictable swings in stress and emotion have caused the heart attack rate to be "as much as 10 times that of the general public" according to Dr. Ira Schulman, director of cardiology at nearby New York University.[5] Many of these victims have died suddenly of a cardiac arrest on the floor of the exchange.

Medically, the term "cardiac arrest" is applied to the sudden appearance of one of three abnormal heart rhythms—ventricular tachycardia, ventricular fibrillation, and asystole (see Figure 2).

Untreated, each of these rhythms rapidly results in death. Ventricular tachycardia usually occurs first (as in Darrell's case in Chapter 2) and, within seconds, can degenerate into the more disorganized pattern of ventricular fibrillation, and then into asystole or "flatline." A cardiac arrest sometimes occurs during a heart attack when an artery feeding blood to the heart closes off, causing part of the heart muscle to die; at other times, cardiac arrest may occur on its own. In the hospital, cardiac arrest triggers a "Code Blue," during which a medical team is immediately

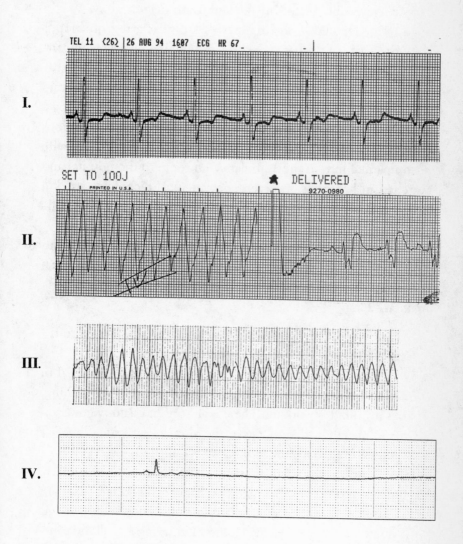

Figure 2: Electrocardiographic Rhythm Strips of The Atlanta Study near-death experiencers demonstrating (1) normal sinus rhythm; (2) ventricular tachycardia cardioverted at the "★" to normal sinus rhythm with a 100-joule shock; (3) ventricular fibrillation; and (4) asystole.

dispatched to initiate cardiopulmonary resuscitation (CPR). This team has approximately four to six minutes to treat the arrest before irreversible brain damage and death occurs.

Largely ignored in the urgency of a cardiac arrest situation is the experience of the patient, who is assumed to be deeply unconscious and unaware. But this assumption is not always correct.

Brent, for example, was stricken with a heart attack and cardiac arrest while cooking sausage one Saturday morning during a Boy Scout pancake fund-raiser. He immediately fell unconscious and was quickly resuscitated by nearby paramedics. His wife accompanied him in the ambulance en route to the hospital and watched in horror as an emergency medical technician stuck a long needle into Brent's heart to revive him. Brent regained consciousness in the emergency room.

He then recalls being transported into the coronary care unit. Shortly after his arrival, he heard a "Code Blue" over the hospital intercom. This was for another patient whom, he believes, "didn't make it." Then,

> about one half an hour later, I hear another Code Blue go off. I am lying there thinking, *Who's next?*
>
> Suddenly I see these people running into my cubicle. I'm saying, "Not me! Not me!" Obviously they can't hear a thing, but my mind is working. There is all sorts of calamity going on and I'm telling them, "Leave me alone! Leave me alone!" I thought they should be looking after somebody else....
>
> I'm watching them from where my head is on the pillow and I'm trying to yell at them, "What are you doing? What are you doing? Leave me alone!" They're pulling my clothes off and I wanted to hang on to my clothes. I'm trying to pull my pants up and I can feel someone ripping them off. I'm yelling, "Stop! What are you doing?"
>
> Obviously, I'm not [actually saying this]. I'm just lying there and my mind is wanting to say it and do it. I asked them later if they didn't hear me and they said, "No, you were dead."

But I said, "No I wasn't. My mind wasn't dead. I could see you. I knew what you were doing and when you were coming in. I even felt you push the board under me."

Medical studies have shown that after the onset of a cardiac arrest such as Brent's, consciousness is not lost for an average of 9 to 21 seconds.[6] Patients may experience sheer panic and fear as CPR begins. Such extreme emotional turmoil may, as with the earthquake and stock exchange victims, seriously aggravate the heart rhythm, which, in turn, may adversely affect the outcome of the resuscitation.

When physical pain is inflicted on the terrorized patient being restrained in bed, an even more deadly situation arises. Laboratory experiments have found that animals physically restrained and repeatedly shocked with *sublethal* jolts of electricity rapidly succumb to cardiac arrest.[7] It is thought that death in this situation is caused by an overwhelming and inappropriate activation of the two emergency biologic defense mechanisms of "flight-fight" and "conservation-withdrawal." In the face of danger, the "flight-fight" response mobilizes resources for massive motor activity, whereas the "conservation-withdrawal" response seeks to conserve energy through disengagement, withdrawal, and inactivity. This latter response, at times, renders an animal less conspicuous to predators (much like an opposum "playing dead" when danger is near). These two emergency systems are mediated by separate neural mechanisms (the sympathetic and parasympathetic nervous systems respectively), which directly affect the rhythm and function of the heart.

Normally, when danger is perceived, either one or the other of these defense mechanisms is engaged while the other is reciprocally suppressed. If an animal accustomed to a "flight-fight" defense is repetitively shocked *and* physically restrained, however, uncertainty develops as to what to do. Such uncertainty may then lead to a simultaneous and rapidly alternating stimulation of *both* the sympathetic and parasympathetic nervous systems as the animal struggles to cope with the threat. This situation, in turn, frequently results in cardiac arrest. In humans, such a lethal situation may unwittingly be created during CPR.

The Calamity of Conscious Cardioversion

One Labor Day weekend, Greg awoke with "simple indigestion." As the day wore on, the gnawing sensation in his lower chest continued. He reluctantly drove himself to a nearby emergency room, not thinking that in his mid-thirties he could be having heart trouble. Although his electrocardiogram and blood studies were normal, he was admitted by a cautious ER doctor. Two days later, all tests remained normal and he was ready for discharge.

> I still had the monitor hooked up to me, which also read out at the nurses' station. I was in a semiprivate room. Both I and the guy in the room with me were feeling pretty good. I was sitting up in bed after lunch at about 1:30 in the afternoon. My wife and the minister were there. I had just finished shaving myself.
>
> I heard the crash cart call for our room and I heard myself saying, "Somebody's made a mistake. This can't be." The first thing I looked for was whether those little suction devices [that attach the monitor leads to the chest] had dropped off, which they do once in a while and drive the nurses crazy—it gives them a bad read on the monitor out there. The other guy and I checked the leads to make sure they were still hooked up. And they were. I said, "Well, I wonder why they got this room?" I was talking to my wife and minister ... with no pressure in the chest, no pains whatsoever.

As Greg continued his story, he began to appear noticeably shaken. The image of a cross between Chinese torture and Saturday night wrestling began to form in my mind. What happened next made my skin crawl:

Then the crash cart crew—the doctors, nurses, interns, and so forth—came pushing this cart into the room and they bodily pushed my wife and the minister out into the hallway and they encircled my bed, pushing me back down. I said, "Wait a minute. I want to explain something to you. I don't think you got the right guy. You've got the wrong room!" I looked over at the guy in the other bed and said, "Jack, you having trouble?" but he was reading a newspaper.

Unknown to Greg, something dreadfully wrong had been detected on his cardiac monitor in the nurses' station but had corrected itself by the time the medical team had arrived in his room. Suddenly, however, his heart did it again and the Code Blue team immediately swung into action.

The head nurse was standing at the foot of the bed when she said, "There he goes!" I then said, "Whoa! Something is going on here!" With that, they slid a board under my back and proceeded to hit me with a jolt of electricity that just straightened me out like a pencil and raised me up into the bed. It felt like every fiber in my body was wanting to jump out of my skin. They finally shut it off and I said, "How many volts are you giving me? I hate to tell you this, folks, but you got the wrong guy!"

Still, no pain, no pressure, and except for the electric shock treatment, I was feeling pretty good. I was still conscious and still talking to all of them.

The nurse standing at my side said, "Close your eyes. You're not supposed to be conscious." I said, "Well then, hit me in the head or something, I'm feeling every bit of that!"

With that, the nurse at the foot of the bed said, "There he goes again." And *whomp!* they hit me again. . . . It felt like somebody ran a rod down through my body and every fiber in my face and hands wanted to explode.

When they shut it off this time I said, "Look folks, you are beginning to antagonize me a little bit!" These are the exact words I used. "I'm about ready to come out of this bed!" I said. "I don't like what you're doing to me!"

What Greg experienced has been termed the "calamity of conscious cardioversion." Dr. Peter Kowey, consulting cardiologist at the Medical College of Pennsylvania, writes of this disturbing experience in his own patients:

> [J]udging from interviews carried out on our referral service, patients have been and are being shocked in an awake state with an alarming frequency.... Frequently they lose hope and express a desire to die rather than be cardioverted again. The physician and nurses are perceived as enemies who inflict pain rather than allies who relieve suffering. One patient remarked, "That's how our society executes criminals." Sleeplessness, nightmares, night terrors, somatic complaints, panic attacks, depression and agitation are all common in these patients, who frequently require psychiatric consultation and many on a long-term basis.[8]

Others have described it "like having everything torn out of your insides" or "like a minor tremor which pulls one's body apart from the inside."[9]

These terrifying experiences, similar to those known to precipitate a cardiac arrest, most certainly could be expected to aggravate such an arrest already in progress. But then, for Brent and Greg, something even more unexpected occurred.

From Terror to Tranquillity

In the midst of pain and fear, Brent's near-death experience suddenly unfolded. It happened, said Brent,

> after they put the board under me. I was gone [snap of the finger]. It seemed to be an immediate transition. And then every-

thing went, everything was gone—the pain, no emotional feeling, no nothing—and I was up in the air looking down at all
this commotion going on around my bed. I was in total peace!
You can't describe it, it was terrific! It was beautiful—no hurt,
no emotional pain, no nothing.

In this painless, out-of-body state, Brent was then able to witness his own cardioversion in a calm and relaxed manner.

> I watched a man take the paddles and rub them and I was
> thinking, *What is he going to do?* When the shock went through
> my body, it jumped and lurched and I was thinking, *They are
> hurting me,* but I didn't feel a thing.

Greg described his transition into a near-death experience
like this:

> They hit me the third time. As God is my witness, I was out of
> my body and up by the corner ceiling of the hospital room look-
> ing down on the situation. I was trying to figure out how I could
> do that—be up there and be down there at the same time. . . .
> I didn't exactly know what was going on because there was
> a bunch of doctors and nurses around the bed. I couldn't see
> who was in the bed because they were blocking the view. I was
> like a TV camera up there. I was in complete awe of what was
> happening.
> Finally one of the doctors moved from the side of the bed
> to pick up something off the cart. When he moved, I could see
> that it was me. Still, I felt no alarm. I was completely cool!

Medical research has shown that just such a switch from terror
to tranquillity as experienced by Brent and Greg may have lifesaving implications. As already noted, laboratory animals subjected
to physical and psychological stress demonstrate a marked increase
in susceptibility to ventricular fibrillation. Merely moving these
stressed animals to a calm environment dramatically lessens their
risk of sudden cardiac death.[10]

This same effect has been demonstrated in humans as well. For one patient, psychological stress repeatedly triggered ventricular fibrillation. After training in meditation techniques, this patient was able to prevent the fatal heart rhythm with a calm and peaceful mental state. The authors of the report concluded that such an "altered state of consciousness" may be effective treatment for some cases of cardiac arrest.[11] In other patients, psychiatric treatment has been found to effectively terminate episodes of recurrent ventricular fibrillation.[12]

This reminds me of a peculiar habit of mine. During cardiac catheterization, patients sometimes develop severe anxiety and "irritability" of the heart despite premedication with a mild tranquilizer. Such irritability may lead to a cardiac arrest. To allay the patient's anxiety (and to calm his or her heart), I sing during the catheterization. I have gotten the reputation as the "singing cardiologist" by the cath lab nurses, and many of my patients kid me about it. Nevertheless, I have found that a soothing diversion such as song (even if sung off-tune) adds to the comfort of the patient and the safety of the procedure. In like manner, the serenity of the near-death experience may "tranquilize" the heart, normalize the heart rhythm, and facilitate successful resuscitation.

However, not all who experience cardiac arrest want to live: Gene, Lori, Margaret, and Arlene did not want to come back.

O Death, Where Is Thy Sting?

"Code Blue, Room 314! Code Blue, Room 314!" bellowed a voice over the hospital intercom. When the responding cardiologist (not myself) arrived at Room 314, CPR was already in progress. To his surprise, the cardiac-arrested patient was Gene, a close friend and a fellow physician.

The cardiologist immediately grabbed the defibrillator paddles and began shocking Gene's heart with a maximal output of 360 joules. An anesthesiologist arrived to begin artificial ventilation, while nurses continued pushing powerful IV cardiac drugs.

Gene would later recall the early moments of this procedure as a "terrifying experience" that he "blocked" out of his head.

According to the medical record, Gene showed no response after 15 minutes of full CPR and 10 to 15 electrical shocks. The Code team wanted to stop. Gene's cardiologist friend, however, could not let him go and sent for a special high-output defibrillator kept in his electrophysiology lab two floors below.

Amazingly, one super-charged shock of 500 joules from this defibrillator restored normal sinus rhythm. By this time, however, Gene's pupils were "fixed, dilated, and unresponsive," a clinical sign of brain death. It was during this time, Gene later told me, that he

was out in infinity space. . . . What it felt like was that I didn't really have a body. It was like a mind and a soul. From a very far distance I could see a light.

I started approaching this light. Then, as I got closer and closer, it seemed that I was picking up speed. The intensity of the light was like a beam that got brighter and brighter and brighter as I approached it. It was incredible how intense that light was. . . .

It was a wonderful feeling—ten times better than anything else. This really surprised me. I had never heard of anything like this before. It's not like a dream, either. You forget dreams or remember bits and pieces of them, but this was so vivid. I was so overwhelmingly calm and peaceful. I felt so good that I didn't care which way I went.

Gene was tempted to stay in his near-death experience and not to return.

Lori likewise told me that she would have liked to have died during her near-death experience four years before. At the time, she was happily married, in her mid-fifties, and working full-time as a marketing supervisor for a large Atlanta firm. While in otherwise excellent health, she had begun experiencing frightening grand mal seizures—a common presenting sign of brain cancer in someone her age. She was hospitalized for control of the seizures, and both she and her husband were prepared for the worst.

Her admitting neurologist misdiagnosed her anxiety as "paranoia" and called a psychiatrist in on the case. Angered by this move, Lori signed out "against medical advice" and returned home to fast, to pray, and to seek the Lord's guidance. Three days later, she contacted her general practitioner who, in turn, referred her to a prominent Atlanta neurosurgeon. Immediately, Lori felt a "childlike peace" that this was God's will.

A hurried medical workup revealed a large tumor on the right side of her brain (right temporal lobe meningioma). Feeling "in my Father's hands," Lori was taken to the operating room for seven hours of surgery during which she had her cardiac arrest and subsequent near-death experience. Here is her recollection of that experience:

> I went down this dark corridor. It was like "time to go" down this corridor. It was like the wind and I were the same. Do you ever feel wind on you, or feel wind blowing in your hair? It was ushering me, it wasn't walking me.
>
> At the end of the corridor was this bright light. Brighter than any sunlight. Brighter than any star. Brighter than anything you can think of. It permeated everything. Everything was that light. It was so clear.
>
> My spirit knew that somehow it was heaven—it was glory, it was all the things of paradise, it was God, it was everything. It was life and joy and peace to the fullest you could think and more.
>
> But then there was this barrier. I tried to push it in with all of my strength but I couldn't move it. I could see through it, but I couldn't push through it. I knew that if I just stepped over there, I could stay in that light forever.

Margaret was another who did not want to come back. Seven years prior to our interview, her son-in-law, whom she deeply loved, was dying of terminal cancer in a large Atlanta hospital. One night during a hospital visit, 67-year-old Margaret, feeling emotionally and physically drained, left her son-in-law's room and retired to the hospital lobby to collect her thoughts. Her daughter followed her down and found her with her head bowed in her hands as if she were praying.

According to her daughter, Margaret suddenly lurched forward fully unconscious on the floor of the lobby. A Code Blue was called by an alert passerby and pandemonium erupted. An assortment of doctors and nurses flooded the scene, angrily yelling for medical equipment and drugs, which were not immediately available. In the midst of the chaos, Margaret was resuscitated and transported, unconscious, to the coronary care unit. *She* recalls, however, a scene quite different from that which was going on around her:

> It was so pretty in heaven. I saw Jesus. Oh, he was beautiful. All that hair was gorgeous. I can still see him standing there, long hair and white robes. And the angels were all around there.
>
> I could see children up there, and I was looking for my grandmother. You're going to think that is strange, but my grandmother was more precious to me than gold. But I couldn't find her.
>
> I felt like I just wanted to get by and see what it was like on the other side. The steps were so pretty. I was walking up them, and I wanted to go.

Finally, Arlene had her close scrape with death following routine surgery for an impacted wisdom tooth. She awoke in the recovery room after the operation and heard one of the nurses ask her supervisor if she could open up the intravenous line all the way to flush in an antibiotic. Unbeknown to the nurse, the anesthesiologist had never removed the anesthesia from the system,

> so when she unclamped the line, I got a massive dose of anesthesia. I knew that I couldn't breathe and I could hear them saying that they were having trouble getting a blood pressure. The nurse grabbed my arm and she couldn't get a pulse and I could

hear them call "Code Blue—Recovery." I was very conscious for a couple of seconds that I could not breathe. I had a very fleeting moment of panic and then I just went out. It was the most peaceful feeling I have ever had in my whole life. There is nothing you can even compare it to.

There was something like a moment of blackness and then I found myself walking down a hallway lined with doors. There was a very bright light at the end of the hallway and a voice kept telling me that everything was fine. I felt wonderful and I just kept walking straight towards the light. . . . I didn't want to come back.

While staring death straight in the face, Gene, Lori, Margaret, and Arlene all wanted to stay. Later, this strong desire not to come back left many, like Arlene, with considerable guilt.

When they got me back, I felt a lot of guilt that I hadn't wanted to come back because I had felt so good. I worked with my doctor and my minister afterwards because it really bothered me a great deal that I wouldn't want to come back. . . . My son was two at the time and my daughter was five.

Arlene's guilt was echoed by others, like Linda, following her near-death experience.

I was angry when I came back, and I remember thinking, *If I could just talk to them, I would tell them to leave me alone. Let me be back in that state I was in.*

Later on I thought, *How could I think that?* I had two children, one baby and one three-year-old, and I loved them dearly and had begged to have them. I had even had to leave one doctor who said he wouldn't treat me if I had a second child [due to my Crohn's disease].

So when I later thought, *Why would I say or think that?* I realized it was because I was in such a wonderful state. Nobody would want to be out of that state because it is so wonderful. I had left whatever had gone on in the past life; I wanted to stay there forever.

But, in each case, something or someone intervened in the headlong rush of these four patients to die. For Gene, it was a voice:

It said, "Gene." And I said, "I know that voice." It was my mother, who died a year ago. I had been really close to her.

There were then two lights: a small light, like glowing gases, off to the side and the main light. The main light was real bright. The smaller light was my mother. She didn't have a shape or anything, but I recognized her voice. . . . The main light was probably a representation of God or a superior being. It was a controlling factor, and it was controlling my body or my soul. I just had the feeling that it was God.

And I asked [her], "What do you want me to do, Mom? Whatever you want me to do, I will go back or go forward." I really think I approached the crossroads between remaining here on earth and passing on. . . .

That's when the voice of my mother said, "Well, it's not your time to go."

I asked, "When is my time to go?"

I wanted to ask all these questions, but I knew there were not going to be any answers. Everything just started going back and that's when I woke up on the respirator.

Lori was turned back by

. . . two mighty angels standing in the light. They were holding up their hands, stopping me. I knew their hands had something to do with the barrier. They didn't say anything. It was just like there was an understanding. Then my spirit had to turn around and I was ushered back down that dark corridor. I was sad. The next thing I remember, I looked up and there was [my husband] Gerry.

Margaret was stopped by someone she called "the Lord":

He was standing on the steps waiting on me, but he wouldn't let me go by. He said to me, "There's no room now." I was upset that there was no room for me. I wanted to stay there.

And for Arlene,

a female voice told me that I had to turn around. I argued that I didn't want to go back. Finally, what made me turn around was that the voice told me a third child was coming to me. At that point I turned around. But it was really difficult. I really didn't want to at all, I felt so good.

Altogether, such spirit-like beings were encountered by 30 of the 47 Atlanta Study near-death experiencers.[13] In each encounter, the spiritual entity was recognized as an *authority in control*. Most commonly, this authority commanded the dying person to return to life and/or prevented the person from crossing a barrier and proceeding into death. We have seen this several times already: Darrell was told to "go" back by the "Lord"; Pam was "pushed" back by her "uncle"; Gene was turned back by his "mother"; Lori was stopped by "angels"; and so on.

Less frequently, the near-death experiencer was given a choice to live or to die. For example, Brent, whom we met earlier, discussed his fate with a "voice" during his NDE:

Brent: "What's going on? Am I dead?"
Voice: "Yes, right now you are."
Brent: "What are they [the resuscitation team] trying to do?"
Voice: "They are trying to save you."
Brent: "Will they succeed?"
Voice: "That's up to you."
Brent: "Well, I really wanted to stay a little longer. I would like to spend more time with my family. I would like to see my children through college."
Voice: "Well, it's your decision."
Brent: "My decision?"
Voice: "Yes."
Brent: "Well, I would like to go back."
Voice: "Very well, then, make it happen."

And the next thing I knew I woke up and all the pain was back again and there was a hairy-faced doctor very close to my face saying, "We've got him. We've got him."

Whether the dying person was commanded to live or allowed to choose, the spiritual authority was always perceived to be in ultimate control—control which thwarted the person's desire to die and buttressed his or her will to live. The Atlanta Study survivors most frequently identified this spiritual authority, not their own strength or the skill of the medical team, as the factor that helped them most to survive.

But is there other evidence to suggest that such claims may be true?

Lifesaving Commands

Doctors have reported that a command "to live" given forcefully to dying patients can actually save them from death. One physician and near-death experiencer from my first study stated:

> Since I've had the [near-death experience], I've encountered this with two patients, one who really exsanguinated and we had a little trouble getting the blood started and I flat out told her, "—, you cannot die!" I really think this has an effect on bringing them back, because they don't want to come back. *I* didn't want to come back. . . .

Surgeon Bernie Siegel gives this surprising account in his book *Love, Medicine & Miracles*:

> Once, as I finished a difficult emergency abdominal operation on a young, very obese man, his heart stopped just as we were about to move him to the recovery room. He didn't respond to resuscitation. The anesthesiologist had given up and was walking out the door when I spoke out loud into the room, "Harry, it's not your time. Come on back." At once the cardiogram began to show electrical activity, and the man ultimately

recovered fully. I can't prove it, of course, but I am sure the verbal message made the difference. I know the experience made believers out of the other staff members who were present.... [14]

In The Atlanta Study, I was particularly interested in the observations of Gene, a no-nonsense, family practice physician. To him, God, *not the medical team*, "was controlling my body or my soul" at the "crossroads," and his mother's command to "go back" was what made the final difference.

Further evidence that such a command "to live" may have lifesaving implications is offered by Charlene, a 50-year-old medical records librarian. Charlene had experienced blackout spells for years, yet her cardiac evaluation had been normal. She was then hooked up to an "event monitor" designed to record her heartbeat whenever she triggered the device. Five days later, she

woke up in the middle of the night, about 12:30, not feeling well. I was conscious enough to push the recording button [on the heart monitor] and to turn the light on. It was very scary. I sat up on the side of the bed and told my husband that I was going to pass out. [The monitor at this point initially registered ventricular tachycardia, then ventricular fibrillation.]

My heart felt like it was beating 100 miles an hour. My chest felt like it was going to explode, and I could feel the whooshing sound in my ears—*Shooh! Shooh! Shooh!* "I'm going to die! I'm going to die!" I said, and I passed out.

This is when I had a dream-like experience. It seemed very real. I was lying on the ground. It was very calm and the colors were very, very bright. There was a red Georgia clay and the sky was a bright blue. There was a body of water that was like a mirror, bright, like in the summertime. There were trees around with very green leaves and bright brown bark.

There was a man standing between the water and me, and he was wearing a brown suit. He had short gray hair, and he was talking—but I couldn't hear what he was saying. He looked stern.

Far, far away I could hear a voice say, "Charlene! Charlene!" It was a man's voice. I wanted to get up and go to the voice. It kept calling, "Charlene! Charlene! Come back!" It was definitely not coming from the man's mouth but was coming from way in the background beyond the trees. I wanted to get up and go to that voice. I was not scared. I just wanted to get enough strength to move.

Finally, I remember opening my eyes and seeing my husband with his face right here saying, "Charlene! Charlene!" I felt that, if I hadn't moved, I would have died. I believe what saved me was the love between my husband and me. He didn't want me to die and I heard his voice and wanted to go back to him. I think he willed me back to life somehow, with the help of God.

These reports from doctors and near-death experiencers suggest, then, that dying may be averted with an authoritative command or gesture.

But *how* could this happen?

In my medical training, I had learned the value of medications and surgical techniques to save lives. The part the doctor may play in saving lives through "non-medical" techniques such as those illustrated above was not taught. A few medical researchers, however, have explored this area with fascinating results.

The "Will to Live"

At Johns Hopkins University in the 1950s, Dr. Curt Richter found in the behavior of rats what well may be the counterpart to the human "will to live."[15] Richter observed that normal rats placed in a tank of water would swim up to 72 hours. After their whiskers had been clipped, however, they would give up and sink to the bottom within minutes despite no physical impairment to swimming. The purely *symbolic* act of clipping the whiskers caused the rats to give up.

If, however, the drowning, dewhiskered rats were rescued and *re*tested in the water tank, Richter found that they would then swim as long as the normal controls. Apparently, through these simple manipulations, the rat's "will to live" could be either lost or restored.

Dying patients, like the dewhiskered rats, appear to lose their "will to live" when they wish to remain in the near-death experience. And at times such as these, a command "to live" or "to die" may determine the outcome.

Dr. Clifton Meador from Vanderbilt University School of Medicine studied a case of a physically healthy, 60-year-old black man from Tennessee who had been hexed by a voodoo priest and told he would die. The man subsequently became ill, lost weight, and was hospitalized. Physical examination and laboratory studies were normal. Despite regular feeding through a stomach tube, he "soon reached a stage of near stupor, coming in and out of consciousness, and was barely able to talk." At this point, the man's will to live appeared to have been lost and death seemed imminent.

After assembling several of the patient's kin at the bedside, the patient's doctor, Dr. Daugherty,

> announced in his most authoritative voice that he now knew exactly what was wrong. He told them of a harrowing encounter at midnight the night before in the local cemetery, where Dr. Daugherty had lured the voodoo priest on some false pretense. Dr. Daugherty said he told the priest that he had uncovered his secret voodoo and found out precisely how he had voodooed Vanders [the patient]. Dr. Daugherty reported that the priest had laughed at him, but that Dr. Daugherty then choked him against a tree nearly to death until the priest described exactly what he had done. Dr. Daugherty announced to the astonished patient and family, "That voodoo priest made you breathe in some lizard eggs and they climbed down into your stomach and hatched out some small lizards. All but one of them died leaving one large one which is eating up all your food and the lining of your body. I will now get that lizard out of your system and cure you of this horrible curse.

With that, Dr. Daugherty gave the patient a shot of apomor-
phine, a powerful vomiting agent, and left the room.

Within a few minutes, the nurse reported that the patient was
beginning to vomit. When Dr. Daugherty arrived at the bedside, Vanders was retching, one wave of spasms after another.
His head was buried in a metal basin that sat on the bed. After
several minutes of continued vomiting and at a point judged
to be near its end, Dr. Daugherty pulled from his black bag,
artfully and secretively, a live, green lizard. At the height of the
next wave of retching he slid the lizard into the basin. He then
called out in a loud voice, "Look what has come out of you!
You are now cured. The voodoo curse is lifted." There was an
audible mumble across the room. Several relatives fell on the
floor and began to moan. The patient saw the lizard through
squinted eyes, did a double take and jumped back to the head
of the bed. His eyes widened and his mouth fell open. He
looked dazed. He then drifted into a deep sleep within a
minute or two, saying nothing.... When he awoke, he was rav-
enous for food. He gulped down large quantities of milk,
bread, meat, and eggs before he was made to stop for fear he
would rupture his stomach.[16]

The unhexed man rapidly recovered without any further
medical treatment!

The power of words to heal was also demonstrated in a
unique study designed to determine whether a "positive" or a
"negative" message from the doctor would significantly influence
the clinical outcome *regardless of medical treatment*.

Two hundred patients with viral respiratory symptoms were
randomly selected for one of four consultations: two conducted in
a "positive manner," called a "positive consultation," one with and
one without treatment; and two conducted in a "non-positive
manner," called a "negative consultation," one with and one without treatment.

Patients receiving a "positive consultation" were told, "You will be better in a few days." In addition, half of this group was given a prescription for a placebo and told, "This will certainly make you better," and the other half was given no prescription and told, "No prescription is required."

Conversely, a "negative consultation" was given to the remaining patients. These were told by the doctor, "I cannot be certain what is the matter with you." Half were also given a prescription for a placebo with the proviso that "I am not sure that it will have any effect," and the other half were given no prescription at all.

Two weeks later, patients receiving a "positive consultation" were significantly better than those given a "negative consultation." No difference in recovery was observed between groups with or without treatment with a prescription. The authors conclude:

> In the past doctors treated their patients in a positive and authoritarian manner because of its supposed effectiveness. Historically the doctor himself was the most effective treatment available. Today we like to think that our treatment in general practice is based on scientific principles, although we do not really know how effective it is ... *[P]ossibly the doctor himself is still the most effective treatment available.*[17]

From these reports, it appears that physical health and survival at times rest on words and commands given by an authority— be it a doctor, a voodoo priest, or a spirit figure in a near-death experience. And, for near-death experiencers, the benefits of such a lifesaving command may extend well beyond the immediate period of resuscitation as it creates in their minds the *expectation* that further healing and recovery will occur.

The "Chrysalis of Certainty"

Two months prior to our interview, 44-year-old Ted had nearly died. On a warm Saturday afternoon at about three o'clock, he unloaded a tractor to mow the grass in his ditch. After working up a sweat, he paused to light up a cigarette. "As soon as I took that first draw off the cigarette, *Bam!* the pain was there," he recalled.

Ignoring the pain, he continued to smoke and to cut grass. The pain worsened and his shirt became wet with sweat. At that point, he said to himself, "Uh, oh! I better just quit right here."

Ted called his sister, who lived nearby, and in minutes he was on his way to a local medical clinic. His EKG was abnormal, so he was whisked off in an ambulance to the nearest hospital emergency room. There he was given a powerful new drug to open his closed coronary artery. Then his heart arrested. He recalls a nurse screaming, "It's dropping, the pressure is dropping. We're losing him."

> When she said that, I just blacked out. . . . I found myself in this little walkway, like a tunnel . . . I got about two thirds of the way down it and a voice—a commanding voice but not a demanding voice—said, "You can't come in here. Go back."
>
> I'm a very hardheaded person, bullheaded more or less. I will argue with a fence pole just for the sake of arguing. But in this case, as soon as I heard that, I just immediately turned around and started walking right back the way I came. . . .
>
> I knew right then that I was not going to die. No matter what they did to me, it didn't make that much difference. I truly felt that I wouldn't have gone there and gotten that far down and then been told, "We're not ready for you, go on back," if I was going to die.
>
> There is no doubt in my mind that God was there and involved in this.

A heart catheterization that same day showed severe blockages in all three of his coronary arteries. Urgent bypass surgery was Ted's only medical option.

But Ted had been assured by the "authoritative voice" of "God" that "no matter what they did to me"—that is, whether they operated on him or not—he would live. If God had assured him that all would be well, he then reasoned, why did he need the surgery?

> I said, "Wait a minute. I need to think about this a little bit," because I knew inside I wasn't going to die at that time.

> So I said, "I have a lot of things to get done here. How about we schedule this thing for right after Christmas?" . . . At the time, I had the inner peace of knowing, "Hey, I'm going to be here for a while."

But with some counsel, a nurse convinced Ted to go ahead with the surgery. Since heart surgery was not performed at this hospital, he was transferred with continuing chest pain to Saint Joseph's. The admitting nurse noted in the medical chart that Ted was still not totally convinced that surgery was necessary: "Patient appears to be in quite a bit of denial of his condition, making statements like, 'I'll just go home.' Dr. L. and several nurses explained to him his condition. After talking with patient, he agreed to sign consent [for the surgery]."

Ted continued to rest in the assurance from God that all would be well. Indeed, his medical record attests to a remarkable clinical course.

He was taken to the operating room at eight o'clock the next morning. The surgeon found diffuse atherosclerosis requiring four coronary bypasses. After four hours of surgery, he was transferred to the recovery room.

One hour later, Ted was awake and calm. He was off the ventilator at 3:15 P.M. He sat up on the side of the bed at ten o'clock that night. At four o'clock the next morning, he was sitting in a chair chatting with nurses.

He was discharged in four days.

Dr. Howard Spiro, a professor of medicine at Yale University, describes his own decision to undergo coronary bypass surgery. After carefully weighing all the options and receiving a strong medical recommendation to proceed, he became "enveloped in a chrysalis of certainty" that surgery was best. This certainty created in him, like God's assurance in Ted, the strong expectation of success. "Of course I'm grateful to have had specialists taking care of me," he says. "But after becoming a patient I'm more convinced than ever of the power of faith, and hope, and *the expectation that all will be well*."[18]

Survival in the Last Seconds of Life

Physicians at the bedside of acutely dying patients frequently witness the unpredictability of life and of death. Factors out of reach of our medical skill and technology all too often appear to be in control. For the dying patient, the near-death experience may be one of the missing pieces in this puzzle of survival.

Medically speaking, the tranquillity and peace of the NDE may "calm the heart" to facilitate successful resuscitation. The command "to live" from a spiritual authority may renew the will to live and turn patients back from death. And assurance of survival at a critical juncture in the clinical course may be just what is needed to sustain the patient and to change the outcome of an otherwise fatal situation.

Could these methods be part of God's mysterious ways of caring for his creation? Survival appears to have a spiritual as well as physical component, with the near-death experience being a critical element in the last seconds of life.

And the NDE may be a key to healing on a long-term basis as well.

Nothing in life is more wonderful than faith—the one great moving force which we can neither weigh in the balance nor test in the crucible. Intangible as the ether, ineluctable as gravitation, the radium of the moral and mental spheres, mysterious, indefinable, known only by its effects, faith pours out an unfailing stream of energy while abating nor jot nor tittle of its potency.[1]

—Sir William Osler, M.D.
"The Faith That Heals"
The British Medical Journal
June 18, 1910

Five

HEALING:

The Power of Faith, Meaning, Love, and Family

In the fall of 1990, Gloria began to experience difficulty swallowing and intermittent vomiting. Her weight dropped 20 pounds. She knew something was wrong, but wanted to "get through the holidays" before going to the doctor. Shortly after New Years, she was diagnosed with squamous cell carcinoma of the esophagus—a particularly virulent form of cancer. After a short course of chemotherapy and radiation, she was evaluated for surgery.

According to a leading surgical textbook, only 39 out of 100 patients evaluated for this condition are candidates for surgery. Of these, 26 live until hospital discharge, 18 survive for 1 year, 9 for 2 years and 4 for 5 years.[2] Gloria had only 4 chances in 100 to live 5 years!

Gloria's response to her predicament was recorded in her medical record as one of "shock and disbelief." If operated upon, her death would most likely occur in the immediate postoperative period. Lungs damaged by years of heavy smoking, blood vessels clogged with cholesterol, and the possibility of leakage at the surgical site made patients like Gloria particularly vulnerable. Her surgery carries the highest operative mortality of any routinely performed surgical procedure today.[3]

Gloria was lucky. Her preoperative workup failed to turn up any spread of cancer. And although her lungs and blood vessels bore the expected ravages of nearly 40 years of smoking, she was still classified "operable."

At 9:15 A.M., April 30, 1991, Gloria was wheeled into the operating room for a seven-hour "esophagogastrectomy with cervical esophagogastrostomy." Her esophagus and stomach would be removed and an artificial communication would be surgically created between the remnants of the stomach and esophagus—a remarkable accomplishment possible only because of very recent developments in surgical techniques.

Technically speaking, the surgery went smoothly. To the surgeon's dismay, however, her cancer was found to have grown into her esophageal wall and had spread to two lymph nodes—a grim finding that further reduced Gloria's slim chances for survival.

As expected, the postoperative course was stormy; but with aggressive medical treatment, she survived. Prior to discharge from the hospital, we doctors had the difficult task of informing Gloria of her revised prognosis based on the spread of her cancer found at surgery. As her primary care physican put it in the medical chart, "It is a fine line between being sure she knows the facts about prognosis and the need to maintain hope."

I continued to see Gloria in my office after discharge. As the years ticked by, her health continued to improve. I scratched my head in amazement.

In the spring of 1994, during a routine checkup, Gloria mentioned having had a near-death experience following her surgery. I was conducting The Atlanta Study at the time, so I scheduled her for an interview.

We met one warm May evening on her back screened porch. Her old Atlanta home was quietly nestled under huge, towering oak trees, providing a dense canopy of late spring foliage. An old beagle was fast asleep at her side, and the crickets were warming up for an evening serenade.

I clicked on my tape recorder, settled back in a well-padded chair, and began to listen as Gloria's southern-drawl voice struggled for words. She described a

white, lovely, iridescent light. . . . Just a beautiful, white light. Warm. Very comforting, like reconciliation. It's like you've crossed over. I feel I have been close and back again. I felt close to God, but I didn't see God. I felt reconciled with God, whole, happy, completed, joy, harmony, and unity with the universe. Very happy. Like you were suddenly grown up and not a child anymore. Like you didn't have to be afraid. Like nothing could ever hurt you again.

Her near-death experience occurred sometime in the recovery room immediately after surgery while vital signs were failing. It was the light, Gloria felt, that had left her with a powerful gift of faith, which would sustain her in the painful days ahead.

My faith was a gift that came in and put me in a bubble. Nothing could touch me really. There was this glass ball or bell of faith and happiness. And it was all right if I died.

I don't know why I had been chosen for this gift. The entire bell of faith, the entire encompassment of faith, was all of God's grace. I was being held in the palm of God's hand. The bell existed 24 hours a day. It was deeper than the near-death experience, it was deeper than anything. . . . Without the faith and without the gift, I would not have done so well. . . . I prayed not to lose it. . . . The nurses at the hospital were flabbergasted I did so well. They joked that I was their star patient!

Intrinsic Faith

Could Gloria's deepened faith have been a factor in her remarkable clinical course that defied incredible odds? During the spring of my interview with Gloria, I met Dr. David Larson at a conference in Colorado Springs and he pointed me to a book he had recently coauthored with Dr. Dale Matthews and Constance Barry at the National Institute of Healthcare Research. In this book, *The Faith Factor: An Annotated Bibliography of Clinical Research on Spiritual Subjects,* they had reviewed in detail 158 medical studies dealing with the effects of religion on health.

Larson's team had been shocked to find that 77% of these published reports demonstrated a positive clinical effect of religious variables on health and healing.

Upon returning to Atlanta, I obtained a copy of the book and discovered that these positive effects included "improved general health, reduced blood pressure, improved quality of life in cancer and heart disease patients, *and most importantly, increased survival* in 89% of the studies which evaluated this parameter."[4]

In evaluating the effect of religion on health, these authors emphasized the importance of separating intrinsic from extrinsic forms of faith, since healing appeared to be associated mainly with intrinsic faith. They referred to the seminal work of Harvard professor Gordon Allport, who had defined intrinsic faith as that which is internalized and practiced regardless of outside social pressure or personal consequences. Extrinsic faith, by contrast, is utilitarian, self-oriented, and concerned with obtaining status, personal security, or social goals.[5] In short, intrinsic faith is for real, extrinsic faith is for show.

I found one of the most striking examples of the clinical effect of intrinsic faith reported from the Dartmouth–Hitchcock Medical Center, where the faith and survival of 232 cardiac surgery patients had been evaluated.[6] In the 37 patients with a deep intrinsic faith (defined in this study as one's "sense of religiousness"), *none* died in the first six months following surgery. In those with lesser degrees of faith, 21 deaths occurred during the same six-month period. When statistically analyzed, this difference in mortality was highly significant.

I then wondered: "Had Gloria's near-death experience affected her intrinsic faith; and had this deepened sense of intrinsic faith, in turn, affected her recovery and survival?" As part of The Atlanta Study, Gloria completed the Life Changes Questionnaire—an inventory developed by Dr. Kenneth Ring to evaluate the effect of a near-death experience on subsequent life and beliefs.[7] In it, she was specifically asked whether her near-death experience had any impact in 42 areas of her life. For each one she had to indicate whether her NDE "strongly increased," "increased," "had no effect on," "decreased," or "strongly decreased" the variable.

Five items in this inventory evaluate changes relating to intrinsic faith. Among these items, her "concern with spiritual matters," "sense of the sacred in life," and "inner sense of God's presence" had strongly increased from her near-death experience; and her "religious feelings" and "belief in a higher power" had somewhat increased.

But how deep had this intrinsic faith been taken? The *absolute level* of intrinsic faith was then determined using Hoge's Intrinsic Religious Motivation Scale—an inventory like Ring's that maintained reliability and validity without reference to any one particular belief system.[8] Here, Gloria indicated on a five-point scale her level of agreement with 10 statements relating to her use of faith, statements such as: "My faith involves all of life," "Nothing is as important to me as serving God as best as I know how," and "My religious beliefs are what really lie behind my whole approach to life." Her responses were then assigned numerical values and added together to determine the "depth" of her intrinsic faith.

The average depth of intrinsic faith in a normal population has been found to be represented by a value of 25.87 on Hoge's scale.[9] I cross-checked this result in a group of 81 nonNDE cardiac patients from my practice and found a score of 27.8—very similar to the score for the average population (perhaps mine was slightly higher since it was administered in the "Bible Belt"). However, following her near-death experience, Gloria's intrinsic faith was an amazingly deep 38!

Thus, it appeared that Gloria's near-death experience *had* deepened her intrinsic faith significantly, which, in turn, may have contributed to her remarkable clinical course. But had her NDE affected her in other ways as well?

Meaning in Life

Two questions on the Life Changes Questionnaire deal with possible change in meaning in life following a near-death experience. On these items, Gloria indicated that her "sense of inner meaning in life" had strongly increased and that her "search for personal meaning" had somewhat increased. She explains:

> I very much feel that God spared me for a purpose. I feel I was partly spared for my husband and partly for my grandchildren.
>
> [My husband] Chess and I have been married for 41 years. We have always been close. I don't mean that things have been a bed of roses. We are both very individualistic, opinionated people. But we always have been extraordinarily close.
>
> And I think a lot has to do with being with my grandchildren. I have eight grandchildren. Five are here in Atlanta, and I see each one of them at least every 10 days on a one-on-one basis.

Medically, one's meaning in life has been found to be important in health and survival. Psychiatrist Viktor Frankl, a survivor of three grim years at Auschwitz and author of the classic *Man's Search for Meaning*, contends that man's primary motivation for living is his *will to meaning*. In this, he agreed with Nietzsche, who once said: "He who has a *why* to live can bear with almost any *how*." According to Frankl, this meaning in life sustained him and other Jews through German concentration camp horrors. Conversely, other medical studies have shown that with a loss of life's meaning, mental and physical health significantly deteriorates.[10]

So for Gloria, her increase in meaning in life may also have contributed to her recovery from cancer. And along with increased meaning came increased love.

suffering brings focusing on the love of God & meaning of life.

Capacity for Love

Gloria felt that her capacity for love had been positively affected by her near-death experience:

> I think that I'm a much nicer person. I'm more forgiving, more tolerant. Things that used to bother me about other people seem insignificant now. It's a very growing-up experience. You keep that. It's almost like a staircase and you have gone up three or four steps. I'm more forgiving and grown-up.

Several items on the Life Changes Questionnaire relate to a person's capacity for love. On these, Gloria indicated that her near-death experience strongly increased her "desire to help others," "compassion for others," and "tolerance for others"; and somewhat increased her "ability to listen to others," to "express love for others," to "understand others," to "accept others," and to "have insight into the problems of others."

The giving and receiving of love has been shown to be medically beneficial. In Israel, for example, 10,000 middle-aged, married men participated in a five-year prospective study to evaluate risk factors for cardiac chest pain (angina pectoris). In this study, a wife's love and support was found to be a strong *independent* factor in preventing the onset of angina, and maintained its protective effect even in the presence of risk factors such as advanced age, high serum cholesterol, elevated blood pressure, and diabetes. With a loving and supportive spouse, the incidence of angina was cut nearly in half.[11]

In addition, her near-death experience had focused Gloria's attention on family relationships like never before.

Involvement with Family

Although Gloria indicated on the Life Changes Questionnaire that the NDE had somewhat increased her "involvement with family life," this involvement, noted in her comments above, had become the center of her life. For instance, when her son in New Jersey adopted a third baby, Gloria dropped everything and flew up to help care for the baby that "we" had adopted.

> This last baby we adopted was from a 15-year-old girl who was pregnant. My son said, "I think this is a wonderful opportunity for prayer," and I understand exactly what he meant. This was a wonderful opportunity to get to know God better, and I feel really close to my son.
>
> The girl is just a delight, and my son's other children are a delight too. I spent a week with them when they first adopted the girl mostly telling the other children they were important too, since the other children felt somewhat threatened.

And family closeness has also been found to be a key to long-term good health as well. The California Department of Health Services studied the behavioral, social, and psychological variables affecting the health of a group of 6,848 people living in Alameda County. Social network—that is, the group of people with whom one is "close," could feel at ease with, could talk to and ask for help—was found to be the *most important* variable in predicting health and longevity; and persons with a close social network had a low risk of dying, even in the face of an otherwise unhealthy lifestyle.[12] Social isolation, on the other hand, has been found in other studies to dramatically predispose one to heart attack and death.[13]

In summary, Gloria's intrinsic faith, meaning in life, capacity for love, and involvement with her family were all strengthened by her near-death experience. All of these variables have been shown to be strong predictors of medical recovery and good health.

As I was in the midst of this research, I was stopped in my tracks by yet another study which seemed to confirm some of my growing suspicions that Gloria's near-death experience may have made a real medical difference.

Psychological Factors in the Cure of Cancer

Japanese physicians at the Kyushu University School of Medicine in Japan reported five patients with documented regression of terminal cancer with minimal or no medical intervention.[14] Key to these striking cases of cancer survival was the faith of these patients, all of whom had "completely committed themselves to the fate or the will of God." One patient, for example, felt his cancer "was God's will and I have no complaint about it. Whatever should happen will just happen." Another patient "wished to serve God as long as he lived, that he would be satisfied if his life was taken away when God so wished." Yet another explained: "I was not afraid of cancer. That was because I had my religious faith. . . . Faith to me is not the attachment to life just wishing to be saved, but it is gratitude to God, who saved my spirit."

These patients also experienced deep meaning in their lives. One patient, a preacher, "shed tears of joy" when told by the president of his religious organization to "remember that you are an invaluable asset for our church." Another traveled extensively for "mission work and pilgrimage." And another found joy in recreational activities such as "reciting Chinese poems or making short trips with her friends."

Finally, these cancer survivors were surrounded by love within a close social network of God, church, and family. The family of one patient, for instance, became very considerate and kind following her cancer diagnosis and reportedly protected her with their love, setting her free from many years of a self-destructive way of life.

The authors concluded that their patients' faith and families, along with the meaning and love in their lives, had in some way led to a "full activation of the patients' innate self-recuperative potentials." And this was exactly what I seemed to have found in Gloria's case following her near-death experience.

But would such changes be found in other near-death experiencers as well?

The Atlanta Study

Intrigued by the thought that an NDE could have a highly positive therapeutic effect, I decided to make this part of the analysis I was doing in The Atlanta Study. Forty-two of the 47 (89%) Atlanta Study near-death experiencers returned the Life Changes Questionnaire, and the effect of their NDEs on their intrinsic faith, meaning in life, capacity for love, and family interaction were evaluated. The results were surprising confirmation of my wonderings.

Intrinsic Faith

The near-death experiences consistently deepened each of the five intrinsic faith items. Moreover, the Hoge score for the overall NDE group was 31.5, significantly deeper than that of my group of nonNDE cardiac patients.[15] Their NDEs appeared to be having effects similar to Gloria's.

When Greg arrested while in the hospital preparing to be discharged (see Chapter 4), his NDE strongly increased four, and somewhat increased one of his intrinsic faith items, and it left him with a deep 37 on Hoge's Intrinsic Religious Motivation Scale. His intrinsic beliefs were strengthened at the expense of his extrinsic religious behavior. Whereas he continued to attend church, he "no longer had time for the little country club things that go on in the churches."

Was Greg's faith important in his subsequent medical course? At the end of our interview, he handed me a typed, four-page document entitled "Medical history since 1969." *Fifty* entries were listed separately in chronological order, including hospitalizations for pneumonia, stroke, diabetes, kidney stones, seven heart catheterizations, three bypass surgeries, and two angioplasties. Greg emphasized that it was his faith, which had been bolstered by his near-death experience, that had carried him through this remarkable catalog of life-threatening experiences:

What I observed [during my near-death experience] has brought me through so much. The night before the third open-heart surgery, Dr. G. told me that because of the scar tissue, he was going to have a rough time of it. I always call it the moment of truth after the doctors leave, because you're lying alone in the bed staring at the ceiling and you think, "This has got to be the loneliest place in the world." You think you are deserted. But that's the time I've learned to turn my whole body and soul over to the Lord Jesus Christ. And I've learned to develop an inner peace that guides me through the whole situation the next day. I don't care if it's a catheterization, angioplasty, or whatever, I have found that there is solace on calling on the Lord at a time like that.

Daisy was barely 35 years old when she suffered a severe bout of heart failure associated with a cardiac arrest and near-death experience. In the 34 years since, her life has been full of what she rather aptly named "ridiculous health situations": a seven-week coma from hepatitis and pancreatitis; a major neck operation to prevent paralysis; and several heart attacks. She is known to her friends as "the cat with nine lives." When I first interviewed Daisy, she was recovering from a four-month battle with pneumonia and was still requiring around-the-clock oxygen and home nursing care.

Daisy related,

My near-death experience was so vivid that it has carried me through ever so many things that would otherwise be so frightful. I had this terrific peace and knowingness. God brought me through, and because of that, I seem to have the will to fight like "sixty" when it's needed. It's the most wonderful thing that has ever happened to me. I can just sort of close my eyes and draw back on it.

I do believe that we are here for a reason. As long as he [God] wants me here, I'm going to use every second I have to give the very best I can give, and I'm not going to worry about it after that. As long as God has a reason for me to be here, there will be someone there to bring me through or a new medicine to take me through, or whatever.

Daisy's near-death experience strongly increased all five intrinsic faith items, and she scored a near-perfect 39 on Hoge's scale. Like Greg, she has continued her regular church attendance in the years following the NDE, but no longer is concerned with serving "man or rituals":

> I was brought up a devout Catholic, but since my near-death experience I serve God, not man and rituals. I have little interest in organized "religion" as such. I find I need to draw nearer to God in my own way by study and meditation. Churches sometimes serve only themselves. I find the Bible to be my best help to knowing and serving the Lord. And sharing with other people who have the same beliefs is my greatest joy and freedom. There are no restrictions in serving and sharing the love of Christ, only joy.

And then there was Rae Ann! A spry 64 when we met, she too felt a new commitment to the Lord following her 1991 admission to the hospital "DOA" for severe shock and coma. Her near-death experience, which we will explore later, strongly increased all five of her intrinsic faith items and left her with a 39 on Hoge's scale.

Rae Ann was not bashful about her new-found commitment. When I drove up to her apartment for our interview in the spring of 1994, her car was conspicuously parked in front with a bumper sticker that read "Following Jesus is not a Trivial Pursuit" and a windshield sun screen proclaiming "Jesus is Lord." Once inside, a statue of Jesus and several certificates of church membership peered down at me from the walls.

When asked about her near-death experience and her faith, Rae Ann pointed to an inscribed plaque on the wall. With less-than-perfect rhyme and meter, it read:

Thank you God for being there for me
Thank you God for hearing my plea
Thank you God for setting me free
Thank you God for letting me see
That faith in You is all I need.
Now I know for sure that You are
Always there, because You gave
To me the most precious gift
I could ever receive.
The pleasure of Your company!

After I had studied the plaque, Rae Ann confessed, "I now regret having signed the poem with my name. I didn't write it, you see. The Lord did."

Meaning in Life

On the Life Changes Questionnaire, The Atlanta Study near-death experiencers generally indicated an increase in both their "sense that there is some inner meaning to my life" and their "search for personal meaning" following the NDE. This meaning, as in the cases of Greg, Daisy, and Rae Ann, resulted largely from a closer walk with God and deepened intrinsic faith. New meaning came for other reasons as well.

Jamie was a 67-year-old professional psychic and had been referred to me by another Atlanta Study participant. We met at a restaurant in early 1995, 18 months after her 47-day stint in the hospital for a massive heart attack, three cardiac arrests, heart failure, shock, and kidney shutdown. She spoke in a slow, gravelly voice—her vocal cords had still not fully recovered from the trauma of the breathing tube required during her illness—and told of three near-death experiences that had accompanied her arrests. For her, the second was most meaningful:

> The next time I went, one of my meditating guides was there. I meditate, and he has been with me since I was about 14 years old. His name was Michael, and Michael came and looked at me and said, "Well, hello there."
>
> I said, "Hello."
>
> He said, "Do you know what is happening to you?"
>
> I said, "No." And I didn't. . . .
>
> "Well," he said, "your heart stopped beating."
>
> At that time I panicked. I thought, "I can't live. I can't live."
>
> "Yes, you will live," he said.
>
> He looked at me most sincerely and most lovingly. It was like . . . all the emotions and vibrations you can gather. He said to me, "You are going back."
>
> I looked at him, because I had been so stifled by his having said that I wasn't alive.
>
> He said, "There are five things I want you to do. I'll be with you."
>
> It is very hard right now to talk about it (crying).
>
> The first thing he wanted me to do was to live life to its fullest the best way I could and that I would be taken care of. The second thing he told me to do was to laugh every day and at every little thing. The third thing he told me to do was to lift up my brothers and my sisters and humankind—cats and dogs and possums and puppies. The fourth thing he told me to do was to help people to learn and to enlighten them, to be an example and to teach what I had learned and to pass it on to those who come to me. And that I would know who they were. And the fifth thing he told me to do was to love unconditionally.
>
> Then he said, "You must go back now."

Jamie found great meaning in incorporating Michael's five directives into her professional life as a psychic counselor. When asked what had helped her the most to recover from her lengthy ordeal, she replied without hesitation, "What Michael had said to me."

Furthermore, Jamie indicated on the Life Changes Questionnaire that her NDE "somewhat increased" both of her meaning-in-life items.

Capacity for Love

The Life Changes Questionnaire further documented a consistent overall increase in the eight capacity-for-love items following the near-death experience.

Priscilla was a young 48 when she went to the emergency room with chest pain and heart failure in June 1993. A heart catheterization three months earlier had shown a heart barely able to sustain life. The amount of blood her heart was able to pump with each beat was only 15% of the blood volume in her left ventricle—the main pumping chamber of the heart. The normal amount is 60%.

Her vital signs failing, she was taken to intensive care and given several powerful intravenous medications. On the fifth hospital day, her kidneys shut down, her blood pressure fell to 70, and she twice developed sustained ventricular fibrillation requiring full CPR. During her second arrest, Priscilla was

... in the presence of this beautiful, big, bright light. It seemed to reach everywhere. To me, it was a beautiful color—it wasn't white and it wasn't gold. I felt perfectly at peace. I felt more love than I have ever felt here on earth, and I felt like I was just wrapped up in a cocoon and that everything was perfect and wonderful and that this was a place I needed to be and that I shouldn't be anywhere else.... It was glorious in the presence of that light. I have never experienced so much love and peace in my entire life from any member of my family or anyone I love....

Priscilla was transferred as an emergency to Saint Joseph's hospital where she received an automatic implantable cardioverter defibrillator—a pocket-sized device similar to a pacemaker which is surgically implanted under the skin, connected to the heart with wire leads, and programmed to deliver automatically an electric shock to the heart to correct ventricular tachycardia or fibrillation.

At the time of our interview 14 months later, Priscilla had had no further cardiac arrests.[16] She indicated at this time that her near-death experience had strongly increased four, and somewhat increased four of the eight capacity-for-love items.

Bobby Jean's near-death experience came at an especially painful time in her life. She was in her early twenties, caught up in a destructive marriage, and trying to deal with the untimely death of her father. One night, she "had a total collapse and decided not to live anymore." After gulping down a massive overdose of sleeping pills, she laid down to die.

> I remember feeling a numbness coming over my body and literally just losing consciousness. . . .
>
> Then that part that I know is my spirit was looking down on that body. The body was totally stationary, not moving at all. . . . I remember thinking, *I guess I've died.* I wanted to cry or speak, but that body could not do anything. It was just totally helpless to move or to make any type of sound. There was just this longing in me to cry, because it seemed very sad at that point that I had died.
>
> Then it was as if the ceiling and roof actually lifted off of the room. It was totally open to the sky. A huge figure appeared whom I immediately knew was Jesus. There was never any doubt who it was. It was a man figure in flowing white clothing, very bright, and he had the most kind, loving look you've ever seen.
>
> He began to speak to me, not verbally but through his eyes. I knew what he was saying and he was talking to me and he was

telling me how much he loved me. I felt it so strongly. He was so beautiful that I began to feel the need to want to touch him and to speak. I couldn't do either.

He stayed there for a long time. His arms were down beside him initially. . . . When I reached as far as I could, his arm extended down and his hand took my hand and instantly the spirit part of me . . . entered my body. There was no time lapse.

Instantly I was able to weep. I began to weep, crying, feeling his love. Not sorrowfully, but just out of the feeling that I had never felt that kind of love before, ever.

Then I awoke. I stayed in the bed for hours, not because I couldn't get up, but because I didn't want to. I was so bathed in warmth and love and caring, it was as if I was being cared for.

Bobby Jean recovered, divorced, and remarried. She has had no further suicide attempts in the subsequent 32 years. According to her Life Changes Questionnaire, her NDE strongly increased two, and somewhat increased six of her capacity-for-love items. Prior to her NDE, Bobby Jean stated that the devil had convinced her that she was no longer able to love and to care for her four-year-old son. Following her near-death experience, however, her new-found love reignited her confidence as a caring and attentive mother.

Involvement with Family

The Atlanta Study near-death experiencers were also asked to assess the effect of their NDE on involvement in family life. Forty percent indicated a strong increase, 40% somewhat of an increase, and 18% no change. The only person noting a decrease in family involvement was Rae Ann, whose homebound status had limited her visits with an out-of-town daughter.

In summary, the near-death experience appears to significantly bolster one's intrinsic faith, meaning in life, capacity for love, and involvement in family—all variables which have been shown to be medically beneficial.

But one further question needed to be answered. Were these changes in the lives and attitudes of my near-death experiencers due to the NDE *per se*, or a result of simply having narrowly escaped death? To check for this possibility, I needed to use the Life Changes Questionnaire to study a control group of patients who had survived a close brush with death *without* a near-death experience.

Control Groups

For this control group, I selected survivors of major cardiac surgery. The uncertainty and danger involved in encountering such surgery has been shown to be psychologically tantamount to facing death.

In a clinical study conducted at Tufts-New England Medical Center, Dr. Richard Blacher found that

> cardiac surgery provides an experiment in nature whereby patients are confronted with what the average person would interpret as dying—namely, a situation in which the heart is stopped before being operated upon . . . It is not unusual for our [cardiac surgery] patients to state bluntly that they will be dead during the operation. . . . This represents not only the emotional importance of the heart, but also the unique on-off quality of the organ; either it beats and one lives, or it stops and one dies.[17]

Using cardiac surgery as a clinical model of "near-death," I administered the Life Changes Questionnaire to 32 postoperative patients who had *not* had an NDE. These survivors evidenced a small increase in their intrinsic faith, meaning in life, capacity for love, and family involvement following surgery. Using statistical techniques, I then compared these results to those of near-death experiencers and found that the increases noted on the Life Changes Questionnaire were significantly greater following an NDE.[18]

In addition, Hoge's Intrinsic Religious Motivation Scale was administered to 26 patients who had survived a serious cardiac illness not associated with an NDE. Sixteen of these had undergone open-heart surgery. Their mean Hoge score was 26.2—significantly less than the 31.5 found in the near-death experiencer group.[19]

These findings seem to confirm what I had suspected in Gloria's case: the NDE *independently* affects major changes in beliefs, attitude, and behavior, which in turn promote healing and health.

Other studies support this conclusion. Dr. Kenneth Ring compared changes in the intrinsic faith of 53 persons following an NDE to changes seen in 49 near-death survivors without an NDE.[20] His findings were identical to mine: near-death experiencers showed a significantly greater increase in intrinsic faith than did the nonexperiencer controls.[21]

An interesting study in the German medical literature evaluated changes in the meaning in life in 28 patients following a cardiac arrest.[22] Only one of these survivors reported anything resembling an NDE, and this "patient thought he remembered . . . 'blows on the chest'." The rest of the group "did not remember anything" from the period of unconsciousnes. *Sixty-eight percent* considered their meaning in life "unchanged" following a nonNDE-associated arrest, 25% felt the change was "limited," and only 7% indicated a "definite increase." These results, when compared to those of near-death experiencers, again suggest that the NDE has an independent effect on one's sense of meaning in life.

Postscript

At the time of this writing, Gloria continues to do well after hitting a small bump in the road in June of 1993. Her heavy smoking had clogged up nearly every major artery in her body with cholesterol, and she was briefly hospitalized for a left carotid endarterectomy—a surgical procedure in which the main artery on the side of her neck was cleaned out. Her right carotid underwent similar repair in August of that year. She flew through both surgeries without a hitch.

I chuckled when I read the surgeon's admission history and physical for the June operation. It read: "Mother Nature has caught up with the patient with a series of recent medical problems." He then went on to detail these problems from a vascular surgeon's standpoint: "Severe peripheral vascular occlusive disease, with greater than 90% occlusion of the internal carotid arteries; mesenteric artery insufficiency with compensatory collateral arterial supply to bowel; aorto-iliac occlusive disease; and total occlusion of each superficial femoral artery." Translated, she was a vascular wreck!

But it was his opening sentence that really caught my eye: "This 57-year-old female patient is a living testimony to advanced medical technology." I thought of Gloria's near-death experience and encounter with a light; of the faith, meaning, and love in her life; of her family, which meant so much to her; and of the medical studies that seem to cry out that there is more to recovery than drugs and machinery. I then paused to wonder how much of her survival was due to "modern medical technology" and how much to these other factors in her life.

And there was one other issue Gloria had raised. At the time of her surgery, her son and daughter-in-law were members of a church group in Texas which, according to Gloria, "believe[s] very much in angels and things like that, and they talk about it a lot. It's real to them, you know. I don't mean they have snakes and things like that, but you catch my drift. . . . They believe that their prayer did a lot of good during my surgery, and I do too. . . ."

> *Prayer is the most powerful form of energy that one can generate. It is a force as real as terrestrial gravity.*[1]

—ALEXIS CARRELL, M. D.
NOBEL LAUREATE FOR PHYSIOLOGY
AND MEDICINE, 1912

levitation?
?

*S*ix

PRAYER:

Spiritual Medicine at Work

Thirty-eight-year-old Gary had been having a tight, gripping sensation in his chest off and on for two months. He knew that his cholesterol was elevated—a condition which he had inherited from his parents, who both had heart attacks at a young age. Concerned, he scheduled an appointment with me for a cardiac evaluation and treadmill stress test.

When I first met Gary in the exam room, he was moderately overweight with balding, gray hair. He was extremely anxious.

The exam of his heart, along with his electrocardiogram and chest X ray, were normal. Four minutes into the treadmill, however, Gary developed chest pain along with deep sagging of the "ST segments" on his electrocardiogram—a signal that his heart muscle was not receiving adequate blood due to blockage of a coronary artery. I immediately stopped the test.

When Gary joined me in my office minutes later, the air was filled with worry and concern. It was obvious on his face that he already knew the verdict: his heart was in serious trouble. As my nurse scheduled him for a heart catheterization, I questioned Gary briefly about his Christian faith and then offered to pray with him. He readily accepted, and we both bowed our heads in prayer.

The next morning, I scrubbed in for Gary's cath, donning sterile gown, mask, hat, and gloves. Gary was awake on the cath table and fully covered with sterile drapes except for his head and a 6-inch hole over his right groin.

The scrub nurse handed me the syringe of Xylocaine, a local anesthetic. I unconsciously began my singing routine as I prepared to anesthetize the skin immediately overlying Gary's right femoral artery—the site of entry for the heart catheter.

Suddenly, my song was interrupted in midstanza by Gary's trembling voice: "Doc, I'm scared! Would you pray for me right now?"

Silence fell on the cath lab, and the beep-beep-beep on the cardiac monitor marked off several anxious moments as I stood with three nurses staring at me in puzzled disbelief as if to ask, "Okay, doctor. Now what?"

I had never been faced with such a situation before—a public request for public prayer with others who may not even believe in God! But there was no refusing Gary's request at that moment. Attempting to hide my embarrassment at being caught off guard, I quickly handed the still-full syringe of Xylocaine back to the scrub nurse, placed my gloved hand on Gary's draped right knee, and began praying out loud Ephesians 6:10–18, the Bible passage I frequently use to combat fear and uncertainty:

> Finally, be strong in the Lord and in his mighty power. Put on the full armor of God so that you can take your stand against the devil's schemes. For our struggle is not against flesh and blood, but against the rulers, against the authorities, against the powers of this dark world and against the spiritual forces of evil in the heavenly realms. Therefore put on the full armor of God, so that when the day of evil comes, you may be able to stand your ground, and after you have done everything, to stand. Stand firm then, with the belt of truth buckled around your waist, with the breastplate of righteousness in place, and with your feet fitted with the readiness that comes from the gospel of peace. In addition to all this, take up the shield of faith, with which you can extinguish all the flaming arrows of the evil one. Take the helmet of salvation and the sword of the Spirit, which is the word of God. And pray in the Spirit on all occasions with all kinds of prayers and requests.

At the conclusion of the prayer, Gary's "Amen" resonated throughout the cath lab. I again asked for the syringe and proceeded to anesthetize the groin, never looking up.

Later that day, as I was dictating the surgical report, I began the description of the cath procedure as I had done thousands of times before: "After the usual premedications, the right groin was prepped and draped in the usual fashion. After 2% Xylocaine anesthesia, a #6 Multipurpose catheter was inserted. . . ." And then I caught myself in midsentence and mused: "Should I modify this second sentence to read 'After praying Ephesians 6:10–18, 2% Xylocaine anesthesia. . . .'"

This was just a momentary impulse. The final cath report made no mention of the prayer.

The use of prayer in medicine, nonetheless, is gaining wider acceptance. In a recent *USA Today* poll, 75% of female, and 63% of male physicians admitted to the use of prayer or meditation in treating themselves.[2] Many of these physicians are praying for the recovery of their patients as well.

One such doctor is internist Larry Dossey, former Chief of Staff at Humana Medical City in Dallas. Raised in a Protestant fundamentalist family, Dossey fell away from his religious roots in his early adult years and became an agnostic. Then, he explains, "I had an incredible experience back in 1988. I came across a study at San Francisco General Hospital called the Randolph Byrd Study. . . . I was stunned by this study. It looked like terrific science. . . ."[3]

Cardiologist Randolph Byrd had studied the effects of intercessory prayer in patients admitted to the coronary care unit (CCU) of his hospital and reported his findings in the respected *Southern Medical Journal*.[4] These patients were divided into two groups with similar severity of illness and were all provided standard medical treatment. In addition, one group of 192 patients received prayer from three to seven intercessors who prayed "for a rapid recovery and for prevention of complications and death." Another group of 201 patients was treated without prayer.

After careful analysis of results, Byrd made a remarkable discovery: the patients in the prayer group required significantly *less* treatment with antibiotics, diuretics, and respirators, and had an overall better outcome than patients in the control group. Byrd concluded that intercessory prayer "has a beneficial therapeutic effect in patients admitted to a CCU."

Spurred on by Byrd's results, Dossey, in his own words, "began to poke around the literature, looking for other studies that might corroborate or invalidate this. I was stunned at what I found. There are easily 130 studies that show that if you take prayer into the laboratory under controlled situations, it does something remarkable."[5] Dossey gathered together these studies in his bestseller *Healing Words: The Power of Prayer and the Practice of Medicine.*

Like Dossey, the owners of General Injectables and Vaccines, Inc. (GIV), the largest vaccine distributor in the country, believe that intercessory prayer is medically beneficial. A leaflet soliciting prayer requests is now included with the invoices sent to their 100,000 customers. Four GIV employees then log the requests phoned in on a special 1-800 number by physicians or their staff; and a group of 25 employees regularly pray for these requests. At least two research studies involving GIV are being planned to ascertain the effects of prayer on health.[6]

And in an article provocatively titled "Should Physicians Prescribe Prayer for Health? Spiritual Aspects of Well-being Considered," *The Journal of the American Medical Association* recently reported on four national medical conferences on the spiritual aspects of health.[7] At each of these conferences researchers from prestigious medical institutions presented solid evidence that prayer is medically important. "We can no longer afford to neglect this important clinical variable," urged Dr. David Larson at the conclusion of the article.

Responding to this growing body of evidence of the effectiveness of prayer, Congress established the Office of Alternative

Medicine within the National Institutes of Health, the most powerful medical research body in the world. Here, Dossey has been named cochairman of the Panel on Mind/Body Intervention to further evaluate the evidence for prayer and spiritual healing.

Prayer, Healing, and the Near-Death Experience

In the early 1980s, psychologist Nina Helene studied 20 near-death experiencers and reported her findings in a doctoral thesis entitled "An Exploratory Study of the Near-Death Encounters of Christians." Nina described several cases in which medical healing appeared to have occurred from prayer either during or around the time of a near-death experience. Typical was the case of a near-death experiencer rendered comatose by injuries and burns over 60% of his body when his car caught on fire in a head-on collision. In this individual's NDE, he encountered "God the Father" and a "bright yellow light." In this "very holy place," the man said, "the Lord had His hand on me. . . ."[8] When his parents arrived at the emergency room to identify their "dead" son, the doctors

> had me in a corridor ready to take me down to the morgue. . . . It was 45 minutes from when I was pronounced dead. . . . They walked to where I was. My dad was very serious in prayer at the time. . . . He said, "Nurse. His hand is moving." And she said, "What? It couldn't be." And they said, "Yes, it is." And they came over, took my pulse, and I was kicking again.[9]

The man then recovered completely and is "without scars" 16 years later. Nina draws a connection between the man's survival, his near-death experience, and his father's prayer.

An impressive array of other prayer-related healings are reported in Nina's dissertation, including a case of "incurable degenerative double viral and bacterial spinal meningitis" during which a woman "became totally blind, severely crippled (doubled over), and comatose," and then totally recovered after a near-death experience.

Two persons had malignant cancer, one with a colostomy and another with anorexia, weight loss, and lung cancer. "Neither of these people were receiving any kind of treatment at the time of this remission," the dissertation asserts. "Both said that they believed God would heal them completely. These two participants do not have cancer today [two and three years later respectively]."

Two participants had severe sugar diabetes, one with coma for three days and the other with a "lethal blood sugar level." Both were cured following prayer and an NDE. Finally, three of Nina's subjects had had a heart attack which brought on a near-death experience, and afterward had encountered no residual heart trouble.

Nina was careful to point out, however, that medical confirmation of these claims was neither sought nor obtained. Several years after the completion of her study, I called Nina and offered to check out some of these cases from a medical standpoint. By this time, however, she had lost contact with most of her participants, making further investigation impossible.

I was intrigued, nevertheless, with Nina's report, and with the growing number of studies relating prayer to healing, and decided to examine this relationship myself.

The Atlanta Study

At the end of Chapter 5, we left Gloria describing the prayer she had received from a small evangelical church in Texas during her surgery and near-death experience. Her middle son and daughter-in-law were members of the church, and both they and Gloria felt that the prayer had been effective. And Gloria has done well since.

Was there a connection?

In considering how to approach the study of prayer, healing, and the near-death experience in The Atlanta Study, one issue had to be dealt with up front. Gloria had been prayed for by Christians, while others in my study received prayer from both Christians and non-Christians. And several Christians and non-Christians prayed for themselves during near-death experiences.

Did the religious background of these people make a difference?

In his study of intercessory prayer, Dr. Byrd used only intercessors who "were 'born again' Christians (according to the gospel of John 3:3) with an active Christian life as manifested by daily devotional prayer and active Christian fellowship with a local church." Nina Helene likewise studied Christian cases.

Dr. Larry Dossey, however, dismisses the importance of Christian beliefs in research on prayer. For Dossey, Byrd's study had indeed been impressive, but he questions "whether Byrd may have had a religious ax to grind, a hidden agenda to prove the superiority of his personal religion."[10] Dossey believes that "the traditional, biblical, Western views of prayer" need to be updated, and himself prays to an assortment of deities: "Goddess, God, Allah, Krishna, Brahman, the Tao, the Universal Mind, the Almighty, Alpha and Omega, the One."

"Prayer," Dossey continues, "does not belong exclusively to any particular religion but to a unity of all religions, classes and creeds. Science universalizes and democratizes prayer. It is a statement for religious tolerance."[11]

In view of this controversy between Byrd and Dossey, I realized that it would be necessary to establish the religious beliefs of my near-death experiencers and their intercessors. To this end, I examined each near-death experiencer with a Spiritual Beliefs Questionnaire. This questionnaire was based on the following 11 statements, to which a subject could respond "True," "False," or "?" (for "don't know"):

1. There is a God.
2. There is life after death.

Very good

try EEG electronic signature

3. There is a heaven in the afterlife.
4. There is a hell in the afterlife.
5. The Bible is the inspired Word of God.
6. The Bible, written by man, is fallible and should not be relied upon as literal truth.
7. The Bible is inerrant (without error).
8. Jesus Christ is the Son of God and thus supreme over all other great religious leaders.
9. Acceptance of Jesus Christ as Lord and Savior is essential if one is to go to heaven after death.
10. Nonacceptance of Jesus Christ as Lord and Savior condemns one to hell in the afterlife.
11. There is a Satan (as described in the Bible) who exists today as a source of evil.

Bible scholars don't exactly agree on precisely what it means to be a Christian. But to analyze the results of The Atlanta Study, I had to set up a few boundaries. The only subjects I considered Christian were those who answered "True" to statement 8. "False" or "don't know" identified them as non-Christian. I further split up the Christian group into those with traditional beliefs and those who were more liberal-minded. Most researchers tend to lump all self-proclaimed Christians together. The problem with this approach is that not everyone who claims to be a Christian accepts the teachings of Christ. We all know there are "cultural Christians" to whom faith is not important, and there are devout believers who are committed to biblical teachings.

Non-Christians were further divided into atheists and those who believed in God, based on their response to statement 1.

The highest score possible—a score reflecting the most conservative Christian faith—was 11. To get this, the subject had to answer "True" to every statement except 6, and "False" to that. I subtracted one point for every "True" or "False" response that differed from this, and one half-point for every "I don't know." For the purpose of The Atlanta Study, I identified conservative Christians as those who scored 10 or more points (that means they could miss only one response, or answer "I don't know" only twice). Liberal Christians scored less than 10.

Using this method, 22 conservative Christians, 13 liberal Christians, and 12 non-Christian believers in God (hereafter referred to as "God-believers") were found among Atlanta Study near-death experiencers (see Table 1 in Appendix).

The Spiritual Beliefs Questionnaire, however, was administered only *after* the near-death experience had occurred. To determine the near-death experiencer's doctrinal beliefs immediately *prior* to the near-death experience, each person compared these pre-NDE beliefs to his or her current ones. Forty three of the 47 near-death experiencers (92%) indicated no essential change, with 36 maintaining affiliation with *exactly* the same religious or spiritual group following the NDE, and seven switching affiliations within the same doctrinal category (i.e., from one conservative Christian church to another, one liberal Christian church to another, etc.). Only four near-death experiencers changed categories, with each of these persons changing to a more conservative Christian doctrine.[12] This high degree of constancy of pre- and postNDE doctrinal beliefs is consistent with the findings in my first study, but stands in marked contrast to the post-NDE deepening of spirituality (i.e., intrinsic faith) found in Chapter 5 and increase in religious activity (i.e., church attendance) to be presented in Chapter 7.

Prayer During the Near-Death Experience

A total of five near-death experiencers from The Atlanta Study prayed during their near-death experience.

I met Jake one fall afternoon in 1993 at his one-bedroom apartment in downtown Atlanta. He was 40 years old at the time, wore his hair in a '60s-style ponytail, and demonstrated considerable skill maneuvering a well-worn wheelchair with "Property of Veterans Administration" stenciled boldly on its back. A war injury had left him with two flaccid legs.

Amidst the clutter of his small living room, Jake began describing his near-death experience during a suicide attempt in 1980. Depressed at the time, he had driven himself into the North Georgia mountains and had overdosed on "20 to 30 Quaaludes and several cans of beer." After passing out, he recalls being in a place like hell, which will be described later. In utter desperation, he said, "I remember begging. I threw myself to my knees and prayed, '. . . God please help me!' All of a sudden, I begged real hard and I came to throwing up the Quaaludes."

Jake registered a 3.5 on his Spiritual Beliefs Questionnaire, classifying him as a God-believer, and a 14 on Hoge's Intrinsic Religious Motivation Scale—two of the lowest scores in the study. Nevertheless, it is Jake's firm belief that his prayful turning to God during his NDE saved his life.

Since his NDE, Jake's life has not been easy. He reattempted suicide twice, each time with Valium. With intensive therapy and counseling, however, he had been drug-free for eight years when we talked. He continued to use prayer at difficult times in his life.

For instance, two-and-one-half years prior to our interview, he had badly burned his foot and was hospitalized for intravenous antibiotics. He awoke one night at 1:00 A.M., sweating profusely and worrying about losing his foot. "I said, 'Look, God. I can't take this anymore. I just give this to you,'" Jake told me. "And suddenly all of my fears disappeared. I went back to sleep and awoke the next morning and was back on the road to getting well."

Despite his low scores on the questionnaires, Jake believes God loves him and is looking out for him.

Another Atlanta Study participant, Marsha, had her close scrape with death 36 years prior to our interview. She was a young mother of two at the time. A gnawing lower abdominal pain developed that she ignored for two months. One night while playing cards with her husband her eyesight momentarily failed and she threw away the wrong card. Her husband phoned a doctor, who attributed her loss of eyesight to depression. Later that night, Marsha fainted while holding one of her babies.

The next morning, her husband took Marsha to the doctor. In his office, she recalls, he took a big syringe "and went into the wall of my stomach and he said, 'If I take out black blood, you're in big trouble.' When it came out, it looked like mud. Black, black mud."

She was hospitalized immediately and diagnosed with a ruptured tubal pregnancy and a massive abdominal infection. She went into shock and, according to Marsha, "I died."

> And when it happened, these two angels came down to get me. They never spoke to me, but each one of them took me by the hand and we were going up. I kept looking back and there were doctors working on me.
>
> And I said, "Please, take me back, I have my children to raise." They completely, totally ignored me.
>
> The closer we got, the brighter it got and the music was, well, Mozart never wrote anything that beautiful, ever! And I asked again to please take me back, and again I was ignored.
>
> Finally, we got to the very top and I only saw about midway of the Lord. If I was to give you the size, he was probably a six- to seven-foot person in the sitting position. And I asked if I could go back, and he said, "Take her back."
>
> When he spoke, it was like somebody had put it on a tremendous loudspeaker and it just bounced off the clouds: "Take her back. Take her back. Take her back."
>
> The light was so beautiful! It was so bright all around the Lord, and his voice was so commanding and yet gentle. And he

said only, "Take her back." It wasn't as if I had a conversation with him.

I felt complete peace. I wasn't frightened.

The Lord did not identify himself, but it was just the presence and the angels obeyed. They knew. There was no mistake who was in command.

When he said, "Take her back," I was turned around, and the descent was so rapid, it was like 10 times the speed of going up.

When I got to my body, if I went over and slapped you right now, that's exactly what it felt like. And then I don't remember another thing. I did not wake up for three days. When I finally woke up, the doctor looked at me and said, "We thought we lost you."

When we met, Marsha had been widowed for 10 years and, by necessity, had become very self-sufficient. She has been a weekly attender at a Catholic church all of her life. She scored 9.5 on her Spiritual Beliefs Questionnaire, barely missing the cutoff for traditional Christian; and she registered a deep 34 on Hoge's scale. Her life, like Jake's, had not been easy following her NDE. She had been hospitalized 37 additional times for various medical problems. Still, her prayer during her near-death experience remains vividly implanted in her mind. It was in response to this prayer, she believes, that "the Lord allowed me to come back."

Greg, whom we met in Chapter 4, prayed during a near-death experience which he encountered after losing consciousness from his cardiac arrest.

"Father," I prayed, "I have to get back because my wife and I have three little boys and I need to help her raise those boys." It is somewhat like standing naked before the Trinity and having to plead your case. When you're young like that, you think you're invincible and that nothing can happen to you. But this was something different that I ran into and I really had to call upon my religious beliefs.

Greg scored a 9 on his Spiritual Beliefs Questionnaire (liberal Christian), and a 37 on Hoge's scale.

For 26 years following his NDE, Greg would be hospitalized multiple times as indicated in the 50 entries on his "Medical History" sheet. Throughout these ordeals, he felt deeply that his life had been given back to him by the Lord—a true "blessing":

> Why I've been blessed so many times, I don't know. How the things that happened to me, happened, I don't know. But I know this, if the Lord Jesus Christ were to take me this very instant, He would have fulfilled every request I have made. I make this witness in hopes that it will help others and to convince others of the power of prayer and to not ever be afraid to call on the Lord Jesus Christ. It's the best bargain you will ever have in your life.[13]

The petitionary prayers of Jake, Marsha, and Greg were answered. Jake's life was "given back," and Marsha and Greg both lived to raise their children. Jesus taught that pressing God hard for our needs is proper (Luke 11:5–13) and reflects a faith in his ability to answer (Heb. 11:6).

The two remaining near-death experiencers who had prayed during their NDEs were conservative Christians with deep intrinsic faith. Each prayed for a specific request, but along with the request they prayed that God's will would be done. This is similar to Jesus' prayer in Gethsemane, "My Father, if it is possible, may this cup be taken from me. Yet not as I will, but as you will" (Matt. 26:39). The "cup" to which Jesus is referring is his upcoming crucifixion on the cross. In surrendering his own expressed desire to God's wisdom, Jesus is expressing greater faith in the goodness of God's plan than in his own desire. This seemed to be the approach taken by Rae Ann and Darrell.

Rae Ann, the devout Christian and author of the poem in Chapter 5, described in her near-death experience being "on my knees praying. I was praying to God and I said a small prayer. I said, 'God, I'm not ready to leave my family, but if you're ready for me, I'll go with you.' At that moment, the most beautiful light came and I was in that light. And the peace came, the peace that I never felt before. I feel that it is the peace that we will have when we get to heaven."

Rae Ann scored a perfect 11 on the Spiritual Beliefs Questionnaire and a near-perfect 39 on Hoge's scale. She attends an Assemblies of God church several times a week. God was not ready to take Rae Ann from this life at the time of her experience, and she continues to be challenged with hospitalizations for various medical problems.

Finally, Darrell Pell (from Chapter 2) prayed verses from Scripture at the beginning and end of his three NDEs. Whereas during each of these experiences, he "kept thinking, *I can't die, Lord, because I've got my little girl and my wife*," his prayer to the Lord was, "What do you want me to do?"

The Lord's response was, "Go." And according to Darrell, "I came right back to earth that quick."

Darrell's scores on the two questionnaires were a perfect 40 and 11, and he continues to be a weekly attender of a Southern Baptist church. In the three years or so following his heart transplant, he, like the others above, has had to contend with serious medical problems. For Darrell, these included heart transplant rejections and a minor stroke.

Intercessory Prayer and the Near-Death Experience

When asked if others were praying for them during the near-death experience, 15 traditional Christian, 9 liberal Christian, and 5 God-believer near-death experiencers answered yes. This represented 68%, 69%, and 42% of these groups respectively.

These 29 near-death experiencers then classified, to the best of their ability, their intercessors into Christian and non-Christian groups. As it turned out, Christian near-death experiencers had nearly always received prayer from Christian intercessors. The five God-believer near-death experiencers had received prayer from Christian intercessors 60% of the time.

The remarkable nature of the circumstances surrounding these episodes of prayer are illustrated in five cases below.

I first met Philip in my office for a routine physical. Although 60 years old, his muscular body gave him the appearance of a much younger man. Years of physical labor as the supervisor of custodians at a local university had kept him in excellent shape.

Asthma was the only illness noted in Philip's history. Since a reduction in lung function might be expected given this history, I listened closely to his lungs, studied his chest X rays, and performed lung-function studies. Surprisingly, all tests were normal.

When questioned further, Philip told an amazing story.

Throughout his youth he had suffered from severe asthma. At age 24, during his last and worst attack, his mother was told that her son would be dead in 24 hours. Then, according to Philip, they notified his brother:

> He was a student at Lexington College in Mississippi. He had been called into the ministry at the age of 13. He was what you might call an evangelist. When they notified him, he left for home and got there that afternoon.
>
> He walked into the room and he began to minister to me out of his spirit and into my spirit. I listened to what he said. Some of the things he spoke of, I knew only God and myself knew concerning myself.
>
> At that time, my brother said to me, "I'm going to anoint you with oil and then I'm going to pray the prayer of faith, James 5:14. The prayer of faith shall save the sick and God shall raise you up. If you have sinned, you shall be forgiven."
>
> So I went on and let him lay his hands on me and pray for me. I had not slept in three days and three nights. Up to that

point, I somewhat wanted to die, and I said to the Lord, "Lord, save me and take me on to glory." And then, somewhere between the time my brother prayed and that night, I went away.

When I left, I felt my spirit when it left my body and went into the presence of God. While in the presence of God ... I didn't want to come back. It was unspeakable joy. I can't even explain it. I was in harmony with wherever I was. I was very alert about everything. Once I came into his presence, I felt I had come to the ultimate point in my life.

At that time I heard a voice, and I knew that it was the voice of the Savior when he spoke even though I didn't see him in person. I recognized his voice and he said these words: "You shall not die, but live, and declare my name before the people."

I immediately felt my spirit when it entered back into my body. And when it did, I all of a sudden woke up. When I woke up, I was totally healed by the power of God from the crown of my head to the sole of my feet. . . . I felt super.

In fact I felt so good that I jumped out of the bed shouting. My mother was sitting there by the bed, and when she saw me get out of the bed and start dancing, she started dancing too. We started dancing from the bedroom to the kitchen.

And Philip has been well ever since.

To me, the most intriguing reports of intercessory prayer were of persons praying on the scene while the NDE was in progress. At times, these prayers appeared to penetrate the near-death experience and to influence the person's return.

Rick is a no-nonsense stockbroker in his mid-fifties who has been a patient of mine since the mid–1980s. During an office visit in early 1994, I quizzed him, as part of The Atlanta Study, about his heart attack and cardiac arrest in 1981. When he began describing a near-death experience that he had not mentioned before, I set up an interview and requested that his wife Barbara be present since she had been with him throughout his ordeal.

We met later that week in the living room of his ranch-style house nestled among towering pines in a north Atlanta suburb. He was seated in a large reclining chair in the corner of the room, and Barbara was attentively perched on a sofa to his right.

Setting down a cup of coffee, Rick pointed to the chair beneath him and said,

> This is where it all started 13 years ago. I was either watching the news or starting to read the paper about six o'clock in the evening. It was warm and I had been outside. I had a little warm sweat. Right after that I got a cold sweat. I was sitting still in the chair and I felt a little tightening in my jaw muscle. I said, "My goodness, what is this? I'd better observe myself."
>
> I went upstairs and laid down on the bed. While lying there, I felt a real fast pain in my left arm, like someone had dropped a drop of hot lead down my artery. It just went *boom*, down my left arm. I said to myself, "Uh oh," and I called to Barbara. She got worried and called the neighbors and then the ambulance got here.

The paramedics arrived, suspected a heart attack, and quickly got Rick out the door on a stretcher. With lights and sirens blaring, the ambulance rushed him to Saint Joseph's Hospital. He was admitted directly to the CCU, where he remained stable throughout the week.

At five o'clock on Friday afternoon, the cardiologist who would perform Rick's heart catheterization on Monday came by to explain the procedure. He

> sat at the foot of the bed there and he started to question me and go over my history. He then asked me a question and I didn't answer him because at that time a very funny feeling came over my whole body.
>
> And he said, "You didn't answer me. What's the matter?"
>
> I told him that I had the funniest feeling, like no other feeling that I have ever had in my life, through my whole body.

Shortly after that, I was "stricken," so to speak. What it was was my heart had stopped, my pulse had stopped, and I guess that gave me the strange feeling. In just a snap of a finger, I had no control over anything. I couldn't blink an eye, move a finger. In fact, I tried to move but I couldn't.

A nurse watching Rick's heart monitor suddenly ran in to check whether Rick had accidentally disconnected the telemetry leads from his chest. They were still attached. Rick was in full cardiac arrest.

The doctor took charge, initiated a Code Blue, and instructed Barbara, who had been watching from the side, to leave the room. Rick's near-death experience then began to unfold:

I sort of drifted off into something like a dream. This is a very significant event for me. It is very vivid in my mind. In this vision, it was like a greenish or pale green mist and like a valley with sort of like a mountainside up on the left. It was like I was traveling down through this valley. As I was traveling down through it, a pale, white vision appeared in front of me. I went on past that vision and another one started to appear and it was my father.

It all seemed very real. As I approached this figure, the detail of it improved and it was definitely my father. He called out to me, "Red, what are you doing here?" My father had died in August 1980, and he had always referred to me as Red.

Just as I was approaching him, other visions or figures started to appear behind him at different spots scattered out.

Then, in that instant, it seemed that someone grabbed me from the back and started to very rapidly pull me backwards. It was just like a *zoom*—I zoomed out of this scene and all of a sudden I hear a voice and it's the nurse there yelling at me, "Wake up. Wake up."

When Rick came to, he was staring into the eyes of Sister Ernestine, who had been summoned during the CPR. She asked him in a calm, business-like voice:

"Do you believe in prayer?"

I said, "Yes."

She said, "Well, pray with me."

At that time I was starting to have a little pain in my left arm and in my left chest. I don't think they had given me any injections or anything. I think they had just been working with me on the paddles to revive me.

Sister Ernestine took her hands and clasped my left hand up to her chest and we were praying there. As we were praying, all of the sudden a cooling sensation started right on my fingertips and worked its way right on down my arm and through my chest and the pain was gone.

Rick was taken immediately to the heart catheterization laboratory where his heart was found to be failing. A cardiac surgeon was summoned and he was sent directly to the operating room.

Barbara, who had been listening all this time to Rick retelling his story, broke her silence. She was quick to point out that the cardiac arrest occurred on Good Friday, and that her presence in his room that afternoon was all a part of God's plan:

I remember the doctor questioning him. I was sitting right beside him in a chair by the bed looking at the doctor and listening to him.

Then Rick did stop. He halted. It wasn't like him because it wasn't a difficult question he had been asked.

The doctor then asked, "Mr. Bowers, you don't look like you are feeling too well. Is something the matter?"

He said, "I don't feel too well." And then he didn't say anything.

The nurse ran in and said, "Did Mr. Bowers pull out a wire?"

I turned and looked at him and his eyes had rolled back into his head. You could still see part of them.

The doctor said, "Mrs. Bowers, would you please leave the room?"

I didn't ask any questions because I knew what had happened. I knew my husband had died and that they needed to revive him.

Barbara hurriedly walked down the hall to the elevators and began to pace back and forth. In those anxious moments, she reflected on the week's events:

When I had followed him down in the ambulance, I had prayed the whole way for God to please just give me a Scripture so that I would know how I had to stand in this emergency; so I would know what kind of struggle I was against.

I just said, "God, I trust you. I really trust you."

I had tears coming down, I was just bawling as I was driving. "Is he going to live or is he going to die? I need to know how I've got to stand. I need you to prepare my heart for whatever."

I could see him sitting up in the back of the ambulance as I was following the ambulance, and we were going 70 or 75 miles an hour. I had left the children with the neighbors.

Before I had left, my daughter had run in the house and grabbed my Bible and said, "Here, Mom, I know you want this." I hadn't asked her, she just got it. As I was driving, the thought came to me that this was not his time. I knew it was God telling me this, and it gave me peace.

When I got to the hospital, it took them 30 minutes or so to get him settled before I could see him. During that time I tried to focus on the Word. I'm used to praying the Word of God for other people in emergencies and I always just wait on the Lord to just get the Word and for how to pray.

I was sitting there, and I got very anxious all of a sudden, and this little piece of paper fell out of the Bible. It was a tract that had been given to me the weekend or two before by my daughter's godmother. I had never read it.

I started reading it and I began to focus on it. It was like the whole thing was a prayer for my husband. It was all Scripture. I started praying it. When I had finished, it was like someone had just reworked my emotional insides. I was totally calm. I felt really high. It was God's grace just pouring out. I had a real peace. I was real settled.

God had given me Scripture all week long and it kept coming back to me. I hadn't worried about Rick, hadn't thought about him dying. I just knew everything was fine. He was going to go home.

As Barbara continued to anxiously wait beside the elevators, she was comforted by this assurance that God had given her that Rick would survive. But she was puzzled over her husband's sudden turn for the worse. Had she misread God's plan for Rick? She then caught a glimpse of Sister Ernestine hurrying down the hall.

I knew she was a woman of prayer, because we had had a conversation about it earlier. I'm sure she went into the room with Rick and I'm sure she was praying like I was praying for his life. At least there were two in agreement praying for his life. I had that comfort and assurance while I was praying.

Shortly thereafter, Barbara received word that Rick had been revived.

Barbara and Sister Ernestine then set up a prayer vigil in the chapel of the hospital as Rick underwent emergency heart catheterization and surgery.

"Who pulled Rick back during his near-death experience?" I asked Barbara at the conclusion of her story. Without hesitation, she replied, "Bottom line, I think it was the agreement of two saints praying, agreeing that this man would live."

Rick agreed with his wife's assessment of the effect of this prayer on his survival and recovery from his near-death experience.

Marty was another participant in The Atlanta Study. She had
been raised in a Presbyterian church in Atlanta and was classified
as a conservative Christian according to the Spiritual Beliefs
Questionnaire. She had been referred to me by her sister, Abigail, who also was a near-death experiencer. Marty's voice
cracked from her emotions as she began to recall how prayer had
saved her 19 years before. She was 26 at the time and had gotten
pregnant with an intrauterine device in place. An infection set
in, followed by blood poisoning and shock.

> By the time they had found out what was wrong with me,
> I had lost all vital signs and ended up in intensive care.
>
> I remember my doctor coming in. He held my hand and
> he said, "Marty, I want you to know that there is nothing med-
> ically left that I can do for you. I want to be very honest with
> you. Do you believe in prayer?"
>
> And I said, "Yes, sir."
>
> He was an older man and he had tears streaming down his
> face. He said, "I want you to pray because I can't do anything
> else to save your life and you are very, very sick. Your whole
> family is praying for you, you have friends praying for you, and
> I'm certainly praying for you, and I would like for you to start
> saying your prayers."

Despite these prayers, Marty worsened. She had a pulmonary
embolism (a blood clot to the lung), became desperately short of
breath, and lost consciousness.

> I felt a tremendous vacuum pulling me up. The force was
> so strong that it was pulling me from my head and I could not
> pull back.
>
> I remember thinking, *Well this is great,* because up to this
> point I had been hooked up to monitors, ripping out IVs, and I
> was in a lot of pain. I couldn't even lift my head off the pillow I
> was so weak.

But now I felt great—better than I had ever felt. There was no pain, and I remember thinking, *I'm going to go with this. This is wonderful.*

Then all of a sudden something kicked in and told me that this was it: I was dying. I knew it, but it wasn't a sad experience, it was wonderful. I never thought how young I was, about my two children, or my husband. I just wanted to go with this wonderful, wonderful feeling.

To describe it now, I would say that if you have ever been in a state of total physical and mental exhaustion and you go to sleep, and you are so relaxed that everything around you is somewhat distant, and you feel so wonderful that you just want to stay there, I would multiply that about 1000 times.

I wanted to go with that wonderful feeling. I know that everyone talks about the light, but I never saw that. And I never looked down and saw my body like I've heard people talk about.

The next thing that happened was that something clicked in my head and I said, "Wait a minute. I'm young, I've got two kids, I've got a husband."

Then the force started pulling me at the other end.

So it was back and forth, this back-and-forth pull. I really couldn't decide at that point where I wanted to go.

The next thing I remember was wanting to stay. I started going with the force that was going down. I knew I was being given a choice of life or death. But I wasn't afraid.

So I kept pulling down, pulling down, and finally that was all that there was, the pull downward.

The next thing I remember, I was in the eyes of my husband. He was kneeling at the bed praying for me and crying. They had pronounced me clinically dead. That's why he had come into the room. There were no vital signs, the priest was there, the whole family had been called.

I opened my eyes and looked at him and he said, "Don't die. Please don't die."

And I said, "I'm not going anywhere."

From that point on I was completely well. The doctor came in and said there was no answer for it. He had no medical explanation. I had not been even able to lift my head off the pillow. Everything completely changed and I was completely healed.

Finally, Bobby Jean, a conservative Christian, encountered her first near-death experience in her early twenties during a drug overdose (see Chapter 5). Later in life, she was hospitalized with carcinoid syndrome—a slow-growing tumor of the gastrointestinal tract which often metastasizes to other organs. She nearly died from an X-ray procedure during which she was injected with iodine-containing contrast material.

They didn't know that I was allergic to iodine, and I had a terrible reaction to it.

My husband was beside my bed. He had had to endure a wife with a long and difficult illness. When I had this reaction, I think that he thought that I was going to die, and he probably thought that that would be good since it would give him some rest. He was not as spiritually mature as he is now. Any time before he would run and get a nurse, but this time he didn't.

We both noticed that I was having this weird coloring, very red and splotchy, and then I began to turn blue. He let it happen and did not get any help. I wasn't fighting either, because I wanted to give up.

At that time, my spirit left my body and began to witness a completely still body that had turned blue on the bed. My husband was beside the bed. He didn't say anything, but he did bow his head and begin to pray.

I remember his prayers. He was asking God to forgive him for his feelings, for being tired, for being unwilling to serve me.

He wanted to be a servant and he realized that he wasn't being one. He asked God to help him and asked God to bring me back.

The interesting part to me was what I felt. It would be hard to understand unless you knew how attached I am to my family. Being the oldest child, I'm very attached to all of my siblings, and I absolutely adored my son, absolutely adored my husband, and I never thought I would ever want to be separated from any of them for any reason. However, after my spirit left my body I was totally indifferent to what my husband was experiencing and totally indifferent to any of my surroundings. I had no desire to return whatsoever.

I began to travel upward and toward light—a tremendous light and peace. So much peace, in fact, that I wanted to stay there, I wanted to be there.

Still, I was also aware of what was happening down there next to my body and of the prayers of my husband. I saw him break down and sob and beg God to please not take me home, and to tell God that he needed me.

I found out later that he was by my bed praying for a couple of hours.

After spending some time—I didn't know how much time—in that peace and light and comfort, the spirit returned to my body. Then I got stronger and stronger.

Prayer, Survival, and the Near-Death Experience

In The Atlanta Study, petitionary and intercessory prayer were common accompaniments of a near-death experience. Did these prayers work? Is Christian prayer more effective than its non-Christian counterpart?

To scientifically answer these questions, all persons undergoing a near-death experience would need to be evaluated. Obviously, many near-death experiencers do not return to describe their prayers. *Only* survivors were interviewed. Thus, the effectiveness of prayer, Christian or not, in promoting physical survival in this situation cannot be accurately determined. I did find, however, that the permanent and total cures of chronic physical illness reported by Nina Helene in praying and prayed-for near-death experiencers were infrequent.

Some claim, however, that Byrd's study, using Christian intercessors and strict, randomized, double-blind techniques, is evidence that Christian prayer is superior in this regard. Siang-Yang Tan, associate professor of psychology at Fuller Theological Seminary, counters these assertions with the insightful observation that Byrd's study did *not* include control groups praying to other deities, thus the superiority of praying to the God of the Bible was not established, only the superiority of praying to *a* god over not praying at all.[14]

Dr. Dale Matthews, associate professor of medicine at Georgetown University Medical Center, concurs: "While science has demonstrated that being devout provides more health benefits than not being devout, we haven't shown that being a devout Christian will made you healthier than being a devout Buddhist. Christians, in general, are not healthier than non-Christians."[16]

Does this mean, then, that Larry Dossey's approach to prayer is correct? Does it make no difference what we believe or to which deity we pray?

J. I. Packer is a professor of theology at Regent College in Vancouver, British Columbia, and a senior editor of *Christianity Today*. He is an ordained Anglican minister, holds the D.Phil. from Oxford University, and is one of the most respected theologians today. He analyzes the healing effects of prayer:

> Statistics suggest that any form of prayer by anybody, Christian or not, helps patients recover. Does that make any sort of sense? Let us see.
>
> Just as an awareness of the divine is natural to human beings through general revelation, so also is the instinct for petitionary

prayer in time of need. Everywhere in every era when crises come, children and adults of any faith or no faith find their minds forming the cry, "Please let this (specified) happen, and not the (specified again)." The dictum that there are no atheists in the trenches bears witness to this. The naturalness of prayer under pressure is a fact of life.

So it is no wonder when patients who have asked whatever God they pray to to watch over and heal them, and who are trusting God to do it, relax inwardly in a way that, being natural, is actually therapeutic. And since the true God is in truth very kind and generous, it is no wonder if those who thus reach out in his direction, ungodly though their beliefs and lives may be in all sorts of ways, and that as they pray, their health improves. Nor will it be wrong to read any statistics that substantiate this as witness to God's everyday mercies.[16]

Packer identifies two modes of healing through prayer: an inward form of relaxation (known as "mind-body" medicine) and divine intervention.

John Calvin, one of the sixteenth century's leaders of the Protestant Reformation, undergirds Packer's reasoning:

God hearkens even to defective prayers. For how often did he [God] ... attest that he helps those wrongly oppressed, who yet beat the air with praying to an unknown god? And one psalm clearly teaches that prayers which do not reach heaven by faith still are not without effect. The psalm lumps together those prayers which, out of natural feeling, necessity wrings from unbelievers just as much as from believers, yet from the outcome it proves that God is gracious toward them.[17]

As biblical proof, Calvin references Psalm 107:19–20: "Then they [believers and nonbelievers] cried to the LORD in their trouble, and he saved them from their distress. He sent forth his word and healed them; he rescued them from the grave."

According to Packer and Calvin, then, there *is* benefit in non-Christian prayer. But is this benefit a mind-body reaction, an answer from God, or both?

Former Surgeon General and Christian Dr. C. Everett Koop responds, "There is a point beyond which you cannot go in proving faith and proving prayer. You have to remember that both are very personal things and whether it is divine intervention or whether it is mind-body medicine that gets you better, you will never really be sure."[18]

But perhaps "getting better" misses the real point in this debate. I met Sharon Fish at a conference in Atlanta in the fall of 1995. At the time, she was a doctoral student at the University of Rochester School of Nursing. Her research interest is prayer. In an article entitled "Can Research *Prove* That God Answers Prayer?" she writes:

> Simplistic cause and effect conceptualizations of prayer should also be questioned with respect to research.... Scripture clearly tells us to pray, and that God hears and answers both personal and intercessory prayer, but in accordance with his good and perfect will, not ours alone. Unlike the independent variable of prayer that we can manipulate in intervention studies, God cannot be manipulated. God is not a genie; prayer is not magic but simply obedience to what Scripture tells us to do. A closer relationship with God and a greater sense of trust are outcome measures that consistently seem to result from personal or petitionary prayer for persons, regardless of whether immediate healing or specific answers to prayer actually occur.... Measuring these outcomes can also be a fruitful avenue of research related to the effects of prayer.[19]

Taking my cue from Sharon, I tabulated Hoge's scores of the 29 near-death experiencers who prayed or were prayed for, and compared them to those of unprayed-for near-death experiencers. Overall, the prayer group ended up "closer to God" than the nonprayer group, although this difference was statistically not significant. Within the prayer group, however, conservative Christian near-death experiencers were significantly "closer to God" than the combined group of liberal Christians and God-believers.[20] These results suggest that this outcome variable may be fertile ground for future study in the effectiveness of prayer.

But whether we evaluate physical survival or closeness to God following a near-death experience, Packer, Calvin, and the other Christians above are *not* suggesting that just any god will do in what matters most.

To this we turn next.

The loudest reaction against *Life After Life* and its successors comes from conservative Christians who see these books as a Satanic trick, designed to lull us into a false sense of security about the future life, to lure us into occult practices such as astral projection, to beguile us into accepting the advances of demons disguised as departed spirits, and to sell us a secular (but fundamentally diabolic) bill of goods about salvation without Christ.[1]

—CAROL ZALESKI, PH.D.
ASSISTANT PROFESSOR,
DEPARTMENT OF RELIGION AND BIBLICAL LITERATURE
SMITH COLLEGE

Seven

CHURCH:

Battleground for the NDE

It all started one warm, fall weekend in Charlottesville, Virginia, in November 1977. A group of eight to 10 persons interested in the near-death experience had been called together by Raymond Moody to exchange ideas on NDE research. Moody's book, *Life After Life*, was still on the bestseller list, and we represented the small handful of scientists who were beginning independent research into this fascinating phenomenon.

As we each flew in that Friday afternoon—Bruce Greyson from Michigan, Ken Ring from Connecticut, Sarah Kreutziger and I from Florida, and others—we had little idea that this weekend would lead to an association that would shape the world's understanding of the near-death experience for decades to come. We gathered at Raymond's house, a picture-perfect Hansel and Gretel cottage, and I'll never forget my first impressions when I walked through the front door.

My eye caught a glimpse of a man in the corner of the pine-paneled parlor, rocking back and forth in a brightly painted white wicker rocker and listening attentively as others noisily conversed around him.

Sensing that this may be the man about whom I had heard and read so much, I immediately walked over and introduced myself.

"Are you Dr. Moody?" I asked somewhat tentatively.

"No, I'm Raymond," he replied, as an ear-to-ear smile broke out on his warm, friendly face.

And it has been "Raymond" ever since.

Raymond shepherded this small group of NDE researchers through each of its meetings, and by the end of the weekend we had formed The Association for the Scientific Study of Near-Death Experiences, which later became known as The International Association of Near-Death Studies (IANDS), the name it retains to this day.

Aside from Raymond, the person furthest along in NDE research at the time was Ken Ring, a psychology professor at the University of Connecticut. Ken's full beard and long, brown curly hair would have given him the appearance of an Old Testament prophet if it hadn't been for the blue jeans and brown penny loafers he was wearing at the time. I took an immediate liking to Ken, and we talked long into the night about our plans to unravel the secrets of the near-death experience.

Ken completed his first book, *Life at Death: A Scientific Investigation of the Near-Death Experience,* in 1979. In reporting the results of his study of 102 near-death experiences, he made it clear in the book's preface that his "interest from the start has been to examine near-death experiences from a scientific point of view. . . ." His hope was that the book would meet "the criteria of scientific inquiry."[2]

It did, and with it Ken wondered if his research into the NDE was finished. Then in May 1980, he was introduced to the teachings of Père Teilhard de Chardin, a Jesuit priest and paleontologist, during a lecture at the Academy of Religion and Psychical Research in Chicago. Teilhard de Chardin wrote *The Phenomenon of Man,* in which, according to Ken, he

> argued that human evolution was headed toward a transhuman state he called "noogenesis," the birth of a unified planetary mind aware of its essential divinity. This convergent end state, the culmination of human evolution on earth, Père Teilhard called "The Omega Point."[3]

Ken credited this Jesuit priest's work as being "one of the twentieth century's landmark contributions to evolutionary thought," and it awakened in him the disturbing thought that perhaps his NDE research was not, in fact, finished.[4]

Meanwhile, our organization was beginning to slowly grow and we began publishing *Anabiosis*—"A Regular Digest of News for the Membership of the Association for the Scientific Study of Near-Death Phenomena." In the August 1980 edition, Ken addressed an issue that he correctly foresaw as becoming divisive within our organization: the religious application of the near-death experience. Entitled, "Psychologist comments on the need to keep religious bias out of near-death research," this piece was straight from Ken's heart:

> I don't think that any of us involved in the founding of the Association ever believed that by proclaiming ourselves an Association interested in the *scientific* study of near-death phenomena, we could thereby preclude religious issues from entering our concerns. . . . So let us be honest, then, and admit that co-extensive with our commitment to investigate near-death phenomena in an impartial scientific fashion, there exists, at least for most of us, a deep rooted involvement with the religious and spiritual implications of our findings. . . .

> And just here, I am afraid, lies trouble because there is a dangerously narrow line between questions of *religious import* and those of *religious doctrine*. As soon as we step over that line, we run the risk of both unnecessary factionalism and hortatory research. . . . If NDE research ends up simply providing new swords with which to wage old religious wars, I will regret very bitterly my involvement with this work.[5]

Tiptoeing down this "dangerously narrow line" between religious import and doctrine, Ken assumed the presidency of IANDS and set out to discover whether NDEs indeed led to Omega.

The Road to Omega

Ken's second major study into the near-death experience was published in 1984 as *Heading Toward Omega: In Search of the Meaning of the Near-Death Experience.*

Here, he abandoned his previous efforts to conduct a study which would meet "the criteria of scientific inquiry" by selecting participants specifically culled from people he met at lectures or who had visited the "Near-Death Hotel"—the name given his house, where near-death experiencers frequently lodged.

A highly select group of 20 or so near-death experiencers was interviewed by Ken "to glean the real, hidden meaning of these NDEs." These interviews consisted of "informal but far-ranging conversations" during which "strong feelings of love" were exchanged—emotions that Ken later admitted "transcended the usual relationship that exists between interviewer and interviewee."[6]

"This was very different from arranging to interview a near-death survivor in a neutral setting on a single occasion," Ken admitted, and the statistical analysis that had been the backbone of his first study was not applied since "the assumption of random sampling is so plainly violated."

"These are not small points, but are major shortcomings," Ken wrote in the opening pages of *Heading Toward Omega*. "The reader must be prepared to consider issues that science alone is not equipped to resolve" and matters not to be "decided by reference to the canons of scientific inquiry." The scientist in Ken had fled, and with it the "dangerously narrow line" between religious import and doctrine was crossed.

Believing his near-death experiencers to be "prophets," Ken devised a Religious Beliefs Inventory to assess *doctrinal views* on such issues as the necessity of accepting Jesus Christ as Savior and Lord to obtain eternal life, and the inspiration of the Bible as the Word of God. The results of this inventory delivered a clear message to Ken: the near-death experience led people away from a "more *conventional* (Christian) religious orientation."[7]

In direct opposition to his statement in *Anabiosis* in 1980, Ken then concluded that

> the real significance of the NDE here may not be simply that it promotes spiritual growth [i.e., an item of religious import] as much as the *kind* of spiritual growth it promotes [i.e., an item of religious doctrine]. [8]

A new religion was proposed—one that would "incorporate and yet transcend the traditional Christian perspective,"[9] would evidence "a marked shift toward Eastern religions such as Hinduism and Buddhism and spiritual universalism,"[10] and, in the end, "make us, as [Manley Hall] says, 'one congregation united in truth.'"[11]

This call for a new world religion was welcomed by other NDE researchers. In England, psychologist Margot Grey claimed, like Ken, that her near-death experiencers believed "all religions are basically the same," and that they had shifted "away from theological doctrines to a more spiritual ideology."[12] Chuck Flynn, a sociology professor at Miami University of Ohio, described his near-death experiencers as professing "many views of Christian belief but in a universalistic way that avoids sectarianism and affirms the worth of all religious traditions."[13] NDE author Phyllis Atwater noted that "two-thirds" of her near-death experiencers simply "cast aside religious affiliations or were never involved to begin with," and that many later founded "metaphysical and 'New Age' churches" and became involved in "mysticism or practices such as shamanism."[14] And Australian researcher Cherie Sutherland claimed that her group of 50 near-death experiencers had achieved an ongoing direct contact with God or a Higher Power that requires no mediation by institutions such as a church or interpretation by the teachings of any denomination or tradition.... Eighty-four percent claim to have no religion, 80 percent see no value in organized religion, 78 percent never attend any church, and only 6 percent claim to be religious.[15]

Ken heavily endorsed books written by these four researchers, and new swords were forged to wage new religious wars.

The Fly in the Ointment

As I followed these developments during the 1980s and early '90s, I became more and more alarmed. In 1982, I had reported in *Recollections of Death* that the religious views of persons encountering an NDE were commonly *strengthened*, and led to a marked *increase* in formal religious activity and commitment.[16] Furthermore, no change in the basic type of religious belief had been found, and no one in my study had professed the type of "religion" that seemed to be emerging from the new NDE reports.

I had to take a second look.

But first, something else had caught my eye.

As a member of IANDS, I was aware of the close interconnections between Ken, now president of the association, and these other researchers. Margot Grey, for instance, had lived at the Near-Death Hotel, had "interned" with Ken, and had included in her "independent" research report several NDEs from the IANDS archives.

"Suffice it to say," Ken later wrote in Margot's book, "that the evidence she adduces in support of her overall thesis replicates mine, and her conclusions likewise coincide with my own."[17]

Chuck Flynn, moreover, included in his work "many of the same NDErs Ken had come to know."[18] Accordingly, he wrote, "I owe the most to Kenneth Ring."

Phyllis Atwater got her start as a columnist for *Vital Signs*, formerly named *Anabiosis*—the official newsletter of IANDS. It was Ken, Phyllis declared, who convinced her to write.[19]

And in the foreword to Cherie Sutherland's NDE book, Ken summarizes her findings as being "essentially the same as those that have been reported earlier by American and English NDE researchers."[20]

Furthermore, Margot, Chuck, Phyllis, and Cherie were all either officers in IANDS or founders of IANDS affiliates overseas.

What concerned me here was not having a friendship with Ken Ring or holding membership in IANDS—I claimed both for myself. My concern was that the independence of the replications of these major NDE studies appeared compromised, and the samples collectively might not be representative of the population of near-death experiencers as a whole. IANDS was the center and substance of most of this research. IANDS had become a wonderful support group for experiencers and researchers alike. But its membership was generally recognized as *not* representative of the general population.

For instance, in *Heading Toward Omega*, Ken qualifies his conclusion that NDEs lead to spiritual universalism in the following way: "Given that virtually all respondents are members of IANDS, however, this result is not particularly unexpected." Dr. Bruce Greyson, the research director of IANDS, has likewise admitted that the IANDS research pool, which has been heavily used by NDE researchers, is "not comparable to the general population."[21]

As I was pondering this situation, I came across a curious thread that was woven into the fabric of many of these studies, a thread that appeared to confirm my suspicions of a subtle bias in this research.

The Issue of Reincarnation

In a 1997 interview, Ken stated that "there is strong evidence that people who had NDEs are much more inclined to a reincarnational view of life; they believe that we live more than once, and that we will live again." He then openly wondered, "Why does the NDE so often lead to a shift in a person's worldview that embraces reincarnation?"[22]

One of Ken's students, however, had already researched this issue. Amber Wells interviewed a group of IANDS' near-death experiencers (many of whom had been subjects in Ken's *own* studies) and found that *none* "claimed to have gained any direct understanding of the nature or process of reincarnation during his or her NDE."[23] Despite this finding, an incredible 70% of these near-death experiencers professed a "strong belief in reincarnation. . . . which tended to follow the standard view of reincarnation as expressed in much of the New Age literature."

Wells concluded that a belief in reincarnation following a near-death experience is a result of "reading, discussions with others, and personal reflection," *not the NDE itself.* And she confirmed this conclusion by documenting that 71% of a "control" group of *nonnear-death experiencers* from IANDS also had a strong belief in reincarnation—a prevalence of belief in reincarnation three times greater than that found in the general population of the Eastern United States, where Wells' study was conducted.[24] Clearly, IANDS participants are not a cross section of the general population and, to a large degree, share common views with each other on topics such as religion and reincarnation. This, it would seem, was the source for the belief in reincarnation, not the NDE that brings IANDS members together.

But this should really come as no surprise. In *Life After Life*, Moody noted that even though his NDE findings do not rule out reincarnation, "Not one of the cases I have looked into is in any way indicative to me that reincarnation occurs."[25] Furthermore, Ken himself had written back in 1984 that

> there is no reason why an NDEr's openness toward reincarnation must stem directly from his NDE. In fact, I am quite convinced that in many cases it is more likely to be a response to an NDEr's reading and other life experiences *following* an NDE.[26]

If this increase in belief in reincarnation is not generally a result of the NDE itself, then it becomes a marker for something perhaps even more important—the bias present in the research reported in much of the NDE literature.

And so it turns out that in *Heading Toward Omega*, Ken found a 66% increase in a belief in reincarnation following an NDE; Cherie Sutherland documented a doubling in this belief to 78% in her group of near-death experiencers; and Phyllis Atwater confidently reported that, "For most, it [reincarnation] becomes as a fact of life."[27]

I then wondered: Since belief in reincarnation is not a result of the NDE *per se*, then perhaps the shifts toward Eastern and universal religious beliefs (which I had not found in my first study) are not necessarily a result of the NDE either? In fact, could the apparent belief in reincarnation come from a turning towards Eastern religions, and could this shift be more a function of NDE *research* than the NDE itself?

Would a study conducted among persons without such influences show similar results?

The Atlanta Study

Recall, once again, that The Atlanta Study did not include members of IANDS and was conducted in a region of the United States that is somewhat different in religious terms from the studies mentioned above. Furthermore, to add objectivity, The Atlanta Study interviews were conducted in a neutral setting, and the religious views of the researcher were not discussed prior to the interview. With this in mind, let us readdress some of the questions raised above.

Did the near-death experience lead to an increase in belief in reincarnation? On the Life Changes Questionnaire, this belief "strongly increased" following an NDE in 12% of the cases, "somewhat increased" in 10%, was "unchanged" in 58%, and "strongly decreased" in 20%. These results yield *no net change* in a belief in reincarnation.

Did the NDE cause a significant change in religious belief or church affiliation? As mentioned earlier, only 8% of Atlanta Study near-death experiencers changed their religious doctrine or affiliation following their NDE (see Chapter 6). This contrasts with 30% of these same near-death experiencers having changed their beliefs at least once *prior to* the near-death experience (see Table 3 in Appendix). Thus, the NDE did not appear to be a significant determinant of new religious beliefs in this sample.

Did the NDE lead to a decrease in formal religious activity? No. Church attendance increased in conservative Christians, liberal Christians, and God-believers alike, with the greatest increase found in those holding the most traditional Christian beliefs. This increase, moreover, reversed a trend toward declining church attendance found both in these near-death experiencers prior to their NDEs (see Table 3 in Appendix) and in the nonNDE control group of 81 cardiac patients in the preceding 10 years.[28]

All of these findings are in line with what I found in my first study, and are consistent with Wells' conclusions as well. A belief in reincarnation and in Eastern, universalist religion is *not* a direct aftereffect of the near-death experience.

One final note: My findings are not meant to suggest that the near-death experience *cannot* lead to an increase in Eastern religious thought. Depending on factors outside of the NDE itself, either the path "to Omega" or the road to deepened Christianity may be taken. All near-death experiencers are imbued with a sense of increased spiritual fervor, but the direction in which this fervor is expressed is determined by other influences—influences I will examine further in the concluding chapter.

But first, other questions loom on the horizon. Many near-death experiencers and researchers have embraced the psychic and the occult. Is this involvement, like the belief in reincarnation, a reflection of bias? Or is it a true aftereffect of the near-death experience?

Many researchers have noted that the NDE frequently leads to the development of psychic powers ... [and] conclude that the NDE can precipitate psychic powers and experiences as if the event itself had somehow opened the door to the psychic world—reminiscent of what occurs in occult initiations of all types.[1]

—JOHN ANKERBERG, PH.D.
AND JOHN WELDON, PH.D.
THE FACTS ON LIFE AFTER DEATH, 1992

*ight

PSYCHIC:

More Than Mother's Intuition

The quaint amphitheater was outfitted with plush, red chairs fixed in narrow, steep rows. I unconsciously picked one halfway up and to the right of the stage—exactly where I had sat for countless hours in a similar auditorium in medical school nearly 30 years ago.

Some things never change, I guess.

I had come because of an announcement I had received in the mail the week before:

April 27, 1995, at 7:00 P.M.
The Center Stage, Atlanta, Georgia
"On Matters of Life, Death, and the Beyond"
Grief Support Seminar
Seats are extremely limited and are R.S.V.P. ONLY.
All seats are $75.00

It was not the subject that had grabbed me, but one of the two speakers. I had not seen him in more than seven years, and I had to go hear what he was up to now.

The lights went out at seven o'clock sharp. A single spotlight lit up the podium at center stage. Moments later, a man with a medium build, dressed in a sport shirt with an open collar, walked out from a bank of black curtains and began to speak in a soft, mysterious voice.

What he said went something like this: "In my experience as a doctor of medicine with a specialty in psychiatry, I have heard a common lament from patients grieving the loss of a loved one, 'If

I only could have five more minutes to be with _____, I would say _____ and things would be so much better.'"

And now there was hope, Dr. Raymond Moody announced. He had pioneered a new form of grief counseling—"evocation of the dead"—and those long-sought-after minutes could become a reality.

Moody described how he had converted an old Alabama farmhouse into a psychomanteum—a place where the living and the dead could actually meet and talk. Here, grieving "patients" could come to an upstairs room darkened with black drapes, sit in an antique, overstuffed chair, and stare into a large, gold-rimmed mirror.

Apparitions and spirits of the dead would often appear, Raymond explained, and unfinished business could safely be conducted in this the "Middle Realm."

The audience was spellbound.

Forty-five minutes later, Raymond sat down in a chair to the right of the podium. With more rustling of black curtains, the second speaker appeared—a wirey, grey-bearded man with a big smile. His name was George Anderson, and he was there, as the flyer had promised, to "randomly select individuals for *live readings* as directed by the Other Side."

George began to call out to the audience—"Is there a John here tonight? Is there a Mary here tonight?" until, after the fifth or sixth name, someone jumped up.

Silence was requested as George began to link up with the "Other Side."

As this dog-and-pony-show trotted on, my thoughts turned to Raymond sitting stone-faced and silent, and to what he had written some 20 years before:

A final note of warning: in my mind, the interesting results of these studies of medical patients who have nearly died should not be used as an excuse for allowing the entrance of spiritualism, with all its bizarre trappings, into medicine. Presumably for as long as there have been human beings, shamans have pretended to put their clients into touch with the spirits of the departed. The history of the fraud and fakery associated with such dealings is too well known (and too ancient!) to bear repeating. The validity (if any) of such performances is best assessed by professional illusionists, not by medical doctors. Near-death experiences, by contrast, happen not in darkened rooms in circumstances contrived by witch doctors, but in the bright light of modern emergency and operating rooms, presided over by physicians.[2]

The Raymond Moody I knew was a medical doctor, not a witch doctor. But that night I felt he had blurred the distinction.

"Spiritualism, with all its bizarre trappings" has long been associated with the near-death experience. Ken Ring, Bruce Greyson, and Cherie Sutherland have all found a marked increase in ESP, out-of-body, and mystical experiences following NDEs. Likewise, an increase in ESP experiences, psychokinesis, auras, apparitions, and out-of-body experiences have been reported following NDEs in members of the Association for Research and Enlightenment (an organization established in honor of psychic Edgar Cayce).[3]

But was this association between the NDE and the occult for real, or just another false connection, like that with reincarnation?

Once again, I had to find out.

Question 6 on Ken Ring's Life Changes Questionnaire asked: "As a result of my near-death experience, my interest in psychic phenomena has . . . ?" Well over half of my Atlanta Study participants answered "increased" or "strongly increased" to this question, confirming what Ken, Bruce, Cherie, and others had reported.

But such an interest in psychic phenomena is strongly discouraged in traditional Christian teaching. Such activity is condemned in the Bible, and in ancient times people who consulted the dead were sometimes executed.

Yet despite these strong admonitions, this increased interest was found equally as strong in conservative Christians, liberal Christians, and God-believers alike.

And just what *were* these experiences with the psychic?

Out-of-Body Experiences

In The Atlanta Study, each near-death experiencer and cardiac patient in the nonNDE control group was asked: "Other than during an NDE (if present), have you ever had a spontaneous or self-induced experience in which you felt as if you were 'out of body'?"

Among near-death experiencers, two God-believers, two liberal Christians, and two conservative Christians described non-NDE-associated out-of-body experiences. Three examples follow below—Veronica, who registered as a God-believer, and Lori and Abigail, who scored as traditional Christians.

I first met Veronica in my office in October 1994. She looked quite healthy at the time—a vivacious, 44-year-old blonde. She had been referred to me for continuation of two powerful cardiac medications which she had been taking for nearly a decade. And she was a nurse and in a hurry—"Just fill the prescriptions, thank you!"

I briefly quizzed Veronica about her history, and then suggested that she consider stopping one or both of these powerful medications to see if she still needed them. Her cardiac rhythm, which the medications were intended to regulate, had been perfectly normal for at least 10 years.

Bad idea!

Veronica hastily sat me back down and set me straight.

Back in the 1970s, she had been having black-out spells and her doctors had diagnosed them as a bad case of the "nerves." She then arrested at home, was resuscitated by her husband, and immediately hospitalized.

After several more arrests in the hospital, Veronica underwent electrophysiology testing, which intentionally induced the arrest to determine the best treatment for her lethal cardiac spasms. In the early 1980s this was a new procedure, and she had agreed to become part of an NBC documentary. With the camera rolling, she arrested several times and had several unusual experiences.

I stopped her right there, and set up an interview for later that week—and I filled the prescriptions with no further questions.

During our interview a few days later, before describing her out-of-body experience independent of an NDE, she told me of an NDE she had had during the NBC taping.

> I wasn't at the ceiling but above the table, and I was watching what they were doing. There was a gigantic glow off to my right—extremely bright. It was bright but muted, almost like a frosted glass type thing. It was twirling around. I was told that if the globe reached me, I would go with it. If I became conscious before the globe got to me, I would live or come back. And I came back.
>
> With the next arrest, I was sitting on the stool at the end of the table. This little cardiology resident, a little short guy, was yelling, "Get me a stool!" It was funny. Here this little guy is standing up, and he's doing this thing, and I'm twirling around in the chair, and I'm looking at him and thinking to myself, *Come on. Let's get with it. Let's just get this over with.*
>
> I was also talking to the TV guys who were filming it. I said, "It's amazing what they can do with the technology nowadays, isn't it? See, she's out, but you watch, they'll bring her back. I know, because I'm her."
>
> I could feel myself; I was real. I was outside sitting around, watching what they were doing. I was flesh and bone.

Then she went on to describe an odd out-of-body experience apart from an NDE. It happened in college:

I had walked into the lounge and I was listening to the Mamas and The Papas' "California Dreamin'" song. I distinctly remember it. I just took off and flew. It was exhilarating. Jumping, taking off, just flying. I know it sounds like Peter Pan. It was almost that kind of "I'm flyyyyyying!" It's lots of fun. I know that I sound like a lunatic, but I know that I flew around a room. I think about it now and know it is impossible but I know that I did it. That's the only time this has happened. It was different from my near-death experience, which was a physical thing.

She then compared these two experiences to dreams of dying she had had during the first few nights after her discharge from the hospital:

I had never been afraid in the hospital, but when I got home, I was shaking so bad. I had never thought about dying in the hospital. When I got home, I was very frightened and I was afraid to go to sleep.

I would have these dreams of me watching myself dying in the bed. It wasn't the same sensation that it had been before in the hospital, and it only happened for two or three days and then it stopped. I would be outside of myself watching myself go through it all again. I think they were nightmares. There were no feelings, it was just thoughts. The ones in the hospital were much more real.

Looking back on it, I can recall one as a strange experience and the other being a nightmare. Definitely. I've gone through this in my mind and thought about it. I'm sure they had me drugged to the hilt. But this happened. It wasn't a hallucination! It just wasn't! Plain and simple. I know, and I have my feet planted firmly on the ground. I'm fairly well educated and I know the difference between reality and fantasy, even if I *was* drugged. I don't tell that to many people because people don't believe you. They look at you and say you are crazy or drugged. But I know it happened.

For Veronica, her NDE seemed more real and "physical" than both her spontaneous out-of-body experience in college and her nightmares of dying. She had been raised in a Catholic family, but was not attending church at the time of the interview.

Two conservative Christian near-death experiencers also had nonNDE-associated out-of- body experiences, and the spiritual interpretation they afforded their experiences was quite interesting.

Lori is a nondenominational conservative Christian whom we met in Chapter 4. She had had a cardiac arrest and near-death experience at surgery. Lori recalled an out-of-body experience she had had while fasting during a two-week period as a young adult.

> I was seeking the Lord, and I had heard and read of other people talking in other tongues and in miracles; and I had read a book, and my mind got to thinking, *Is this really, really God?* I was fasting and I asked the Lord to confirm it with his Word.
>
> As I was studying the Word, I fell asleep. Well, here was my bed and there was the window. It was like someone blew in the window and reached over and took me by the hand. I got up out of bed and I looked back and I was still lying in the bed. We went through that window and over Chicago, over the skyline, and saw Lake Michigan. At the edge of Lake Michigan, there was a great drop-off place. It looked like a terrible pit. I heard people—it might have been spirits—crying out, and they were trying to climb up out of that pit. It was like I understood that there was no hope for them. I just understood this, there were no words spoken.
>
> I was overwhelmed by it and couldn't stand to look at it anymore. I immediately came back through the window and back into my body and woke up.

Abigail, a 40-year-old Christian lay counselor, encountered several out-of-body experiences while in college at a time when she was not a Christian and was "searching, confused and depressed":

I remember one while I was in my dorm room asleep. I came out of my body, floated out the window, and floated down with the fall leaves. I had another where I felt like I was flying over a viaduct in Europe. And another one of simply being in my room and trying to get out. I would leave my body and hit the ceiling. While it was frightening, it was pretty neat to wake up the next morning and to know I had done this, that I had left my body.

These were very stressful. I didn't know what they were. They bothered me. I didn't like them. They were very different from a dream. I left my body and saw my body in bed. That was all in college. I have not had any since I have had my near-death experience.

Out-of-body experiences are real. The significance to me now is that Satan, the enemy, was very much trying to get me involved in anything else other than God. I was searching at that time in my life, and I can remember being interested in the supernatural.

I had had a friend in high school who claimed that she was a witch and I was interested in that sort of thing. I believe that Satan was trying to get me to put my interests and my energies and my beliefs in that instead of in God, because it did not do anything to turn me toward God. It did not do anything to glorify God. If anything, it was glorifying me. It emphasized me and it didn't emphasize God.

But it really happened. Had people come along and encouraged me in all of this, I would have probably said, "This is neat," but somehow I was protected from them.

In addition, one God-believer and one liberal Christian reported out-of-body experiences during meditation. And one liberal Christian had had an out-of-body experience during a particularly moving church service when nine years old.

These six near-death experiencers represented 13% of the entire group, whereas 9% of the nonNDE control group reported out-of-body experiences.[4] Furthermore, these unusual experiences did not become more frequent following an NDE in any person; and, for many, they altogether ceased.

Visions

Visions are experiences through which the person believes supernatural insight or awareness has been given. Visions differ from dreams in that dreams are clearly perceived in retrospect to be fantasy, while visions are felt to be perceptions of reality. Dreams occur only during sleep, while visions can happen while a person is awake.

Each near-death experiencer and cardiac patient was asked: "Other than the NDE (if present), have you ever had a vision (i.e., a visual perception of a nonphysical entity) which you felt may have been a manifestation of the spiritual realm?" Nineteen in the NDE group answered yes, with over half of these positive responses from conservative Christians such as Rae Ann, Lori, Bobby Jean, Darrell, and Abigail.

Rae Ann, the colorful 64-year-old woman with the "Following Jesus is not a Trivial Pursuit" bumper sticker, encountered the vision of an "angel" six weeks prior to her near-death experience:

> My husband and I were sitting in our den watching a Braves game. All of a sudden this angel came out of the laundry room, just through the wall, and marched right up to me with his hands extended like this with a smile on his face. I thought that I was dreaming. I blinked my eyes and I looked at my husband, he was still over there on the couch; and I looked back at the TV, and the TV was still going and the angel was still there. I knew that I wasn't dreaming. In fact, I pinched myself to make sure.
>
> I thought, *What in the world? It looks like an angel. Transparent.* His hair was like gold around his shoulders, and I never will forget what he looked like—he was gorgeous. He had his hands out, both of them. He walked right up to me.

I thought, *What is going on?* I kind of got up in the chair and he stepped back, like he thought that I might be coming to touch him or something. He stepped back and stood there for just a few more minutes. And then he just backed out, just like he came in.

I sat there for a few minutes and I looked around and I didn't see anything else. Finally, I said to my husband, "Chuck, turn off the TV. We have to talk."

He turned it off and he said, "What's going on?" And I said, "Did you see that angel that just came in here?" And he said, "No. I didn't see an angel." I said, "You didn't see an angel come in and stand right in front of me?" He said, "No."

I said, "Chuck, you're probably going to think I'm crazy, but an angel just came through that wall up here to me with his hands extended." And I told him what had happened.

He said, "Well, it wasn't meant for me to see."

I explained to him what he looked like and everything.

I said, "Do you think that angel came after me?" And he said, "No. If he had come after you, you would have gone back with him."

We discussed it in detail. We got up and went to the kitchen table and talked that night for a long, long time. I still was not satisfied, because I knew something had happened. I didn't know why, I didn't really know what. But I knew that it was an angel.

We talked about it every day for a while. Six weeks later, the Friday before Mother's Day, I died.

Lori recalled meeting two angels in the emergency room days before her near-death experience and brain surgery:

I was on the gurney being moved into the emergency room before the doctor came in. I looked up and [my husband] Gerry was looking so concerned and so undone, so worried. The words that came out of my mouth were, "Gerry, don't you be afraid. There are two mighty angels here. Nothing is going to happen."

I saw two big men of light. The two angels were standing at the end of the gurney, between the gurney and the doors. They were almost as tall as this ceiling. They were men of light. You could see arms and legs and a head.

They were too blinding to look at—like trying to look at the sunlight, you couldn't look at it. I knew they were there, but it hurt your eyes to look at them. They were just standing there.

Somehow I knew everything was okay, and I had to say that to Gerry, for him not to be so concerned.

Bobby Jean, following her near-death experience from an allergic reaction to X-ray dye, had a vision of a church to which she felt the Lord was leading her and her husband.

I had never had a vision before in my life. I had a vision of a church that I had never seen before and was not familiar with. I felt that I was instructed that this was where we were to go to church, that God had a plan for us in that church. Prior to that time we had been going to a different church.

That same day I checked myself out of that hospital. From this vision, my senses were so heightened that it is hard to explain. I knew that I had to get out of that place to survive. I had gotten worse from the moment I had gone in there. I had to be taken home on a stretcher and in an ambulance.

The Lord, through this vision, had given me a heightened gift of discernment. We found that church the next Sunday, and that's where we stayed and my husband became a deacon: North Jacksonville Church of God.

Darrell Pell had what he termed a "Satan experience" a few days following his near-death experiences, while still in intensive care awaiting a heart transplant.

I took a nap and all of a sudden I saw what looked like a Mexican guy about six foot tall or so with a little black moustache, a cowboy hat, and a shirt, and he had grabbed a pillow and he was coming my way and I couldn't wake up from my dream.

I said, "This is just a dream and I need to wake up." But I couldn't. So then I said, "This ain't no dream, this is a spirit. Now I'm in my spiritual realm, this realm they talk about in church." I'd seen the out-of-body experience and it was as real as real can be, and this guy was coming with this pillow and he was about to put it over my head.

I said, "In the name of Jesus Christ, I rebuke this devil out of my room." And about that time, *bam* [snap of finger] he was gone. Just like that. Just that quick.

Then I was released to wake up and I woke up. Wow! I was breathing hard, but no nurses came in. I thought it would affect the monitors, but it didn't. So I was like, "Wow, this is real. God, I'm going to stay right to you. I'm going to cling right to you. You're my foundation and my rock like it says in the Psalms. I'm going to cleave to you."

And Abigail encountered her vision at age 28 while praying at home shortly after hospital discharge from an emergency hysterectomy for severe hemorrhage and shock associated with a near-death experience. In this vision, she experienced a "presence" of Christ similar to the "presence" encountered in her NDE.

I was praying for my daughter [whom I adopted later] after I had gotten well and was back home. I don't know if at this time I already knew that she was on the way or whether I was just praying for the child that God was going to send. I was in what was to be her nursery.

I was on the floor, on my hands and knees. While I was praying, I once again felt a very strong presence. It was so strong that I was afraid to turn around. I wasn't scared or frightened, just in awe. I didn't know what I would see if I turned around. And I didn't turn around!

This was similar to my experience in the hospital, just a very close awareness that this was very real. There was nothing I had asked for, nothing I was looking for, which made it all the more real.

Since this time, I have asked to see or feel, and it doesn't work that way. God does things his way.

Abigail's prayers were answered. On March 24, 1983, a year to the day that she had lost her first baby in miscarriage, she was notified by the adoption agency that a child was on the way. She was due to arrive on May 19, the due date of Abigail's second baby, which she had lost immediately prior to the emergency hysterectomy. To Abigail, the correspondence of these dates was "very much confirmation that the Lord was in control."

In two instances, visionary encounters were accompanied by the presence of a light. Reports of seeing a light, especially in times of intense prayer, is fairly common. Recall, for instance, Alison Pell praying late one night over the sleeping body of Darrell. She saw a light that she identified as the Lord, and that gave her the solid conviction that Darrell would survive. Alison's account is nearly word for word like one which Nina Helene reported, also a wife praying over her comatose husband and near-death experiencer:

> I looked over at him and I could see a soft blue light over him . . . a healing light. I *knew* that everything would be alright from seeing this. Nobody else could see it. I didn't say anything to anybody. And then right along the railing it was blue and purple light. . . . just a soft light . . . and I knew my prayer had been answered.[5]

Compare these two accounts now, to the one reported by Amy, a God-believer and near-death experiencer from The Atlanta Study, during prayer over her dying infant:

My child was jaundiced badly and I knew something was wrong at the hospital because he couldn't suck. I was trying to nurse him.

Nobody back then wanted to nurse their child. The head nurse told me that the only people who nursed their children were itinerant ignorant Mexicans.

I remember saying, "If it was good enough for my grandmother, it was good enough for me. Now bring my baby to me."

But he couldn't nurse. He couldn't suck. And the doctor had gone on vacation and they couldn't help me.

I left the hospital and shortly thereafter my son started getting worse and started having convulsions. His back was completely in a circle with his head touching his feet. I called the emergency room and I took him in.

At that point the doctor who was going to operate on him came to me and said, "You know your son is going to be nothing but a vegetable when we are through with this. Do you want us to let him die or do you want him to live?"

I said, "Do what you can." I just remember being so emotionally destroyed. I then thought that I had made the wrong choice to let them operate on him, but it was too late.

It was probably midnight and I was staying at the hospital. I just couldn't leave, and I was torn by the decision I had made. I can't tell you how many times I thought that I had made the wrong decision.

After the surgery, I remember just laying my head down on the side . . . and I cried till I couldn't cry anymore. I was holding onto the side of the bed, praying that I had made the right decision, and that if my son lived, that I would do the best I could by him.

All of a sudden this white light bathed my son, and I knew he was going to live. It was just around my son. (There were other babies there in the room because it was where all the critical cases were.) Immediately, I knew that everything was alright. I knew that from that point on my son was going to survive.

I thought I was hysterical at the time, that maybe I had cried so much that I was hallucinating. . . . But I knew, when I saw that light, that my son was going to be alright, and I stopped suffering.

I have never heard anyone ever describe seeing a light over someone in a critical situation and dying. I have never heard of that. But that's what happened to me.

The similarity of these three cases is remarkable, and raises questions about how God manifests his presence to us. Could these accounts be similar to the one in Acts 12:7 when the "angel of the Lord" appeared as a "light [that] shone in the cell" to the sleeping Peter?

Margaret, the conservative Christian who arrested in the lobby of an Atlanta hospital, was awakened, like Peter, by a light several years before her NDE:

I had two strokes on my right side and the doctor told me that I would never walk any more and that I would be in a wheelchair. I was very upset. I remember lying in bed one night and saying, "Please, Lord, help me walk. Help me, Lord."

He came up on my footboard and my room lit up. He stood on my footboard and said, "Don't worry, everything is going to be all right, my child." It was very plain. He looked just like when I went to heaven [during my near-death experience].

Let me tell you, everything has been alright. At the time, I could not speak. My right side of my mouth was drawn. I was living by myself, and I would sit in front of a mirror and I learned to say "cat" and "rat," I took a ball and squeezed my right hand, I drove with my left foot, I walked with a cane. But now I have fully recovered.

In all, 40% of near-death experiencers—10 conservative Christians, 4 liberal Christians and 5 God-believers—had visionary experiences. Only 12 of the 81 (15%) of the nonNDE cardiac patients recalled such a vision. Thus, such encounters were significantly more common in near-death experiencers.[6]

Precognition

Finally, each near-death experiencer and control patient was asked: "Have you ever been made aware of another person's life-threatening crisis (e.g., death, accident, sudden illness, etc.) through 'non-ordinary' means such as 'intuition,' 'spiritual visitation,' 'vision,' et cetera?"

Twenty-six near-death experiencers claimed to have had such an occurrence. This precognitive knowledge was often received during a vision around the time of the NDE—like with Abigail and her assurance of a new child from the presence of the "Lord," and with Bobby Jean's vision of her new church. These precognitions seemed to have been accurately fulfilled. The precognitive experiences of three conservative Christians will serve as examples.

Lori had a premonition of her brain tumor, surgery, and NDE a year before it happened. At this time,

> I was perfectly healthy. We had come home from getting groceries one night. I turned to my husband and told him that I was just listening to my heart and was told, "Get your house in order or you will surely die."
>
> I asked him, "Did the Lord say that to me?"
>
> My husband said, "Honey, let us pray about it and see."
>
> We just prayed about it and forgot about it until all of this happened. It was like a memory on hold. We were being prepared a year before all of this happened, and I didn't know it.

Paige was a 50-year-old housewife who was electrocuted while cleaning her garage with a power washer. Three weeks prior to this event, she had a premonition of its occurrence:

> I had this nagging feeling that something was wrong. I couldn't define what was happening and I said, "Lord, what are you trying to tell me?"

Then one day, while in my library, I had a very real experience. I was putting up books and it just seemed that the Lord was saying, "Would you do anything I ask of you?"

I said, "Well, Lord, I've always wanted to do what you wanted me to do and to be where you wanted me to be."

He asked again and finally I was just talking out loud and I said, "Lord, I feel like Peter: 'Loveth thou me, loveth thou me?' Show me, Lord, what this is. What do you want of me?"

This very strong feeling came. It was as if he was asking, "Would you be willing to be faithful to me, no matter what I require of you?"

Frankly, I thought widowhood was what he had in mind.

I just dropped to my knees and said, "Lord, I want to be willing. I think that I am willing. If I'm not, then make me willing." And the burden left.

Three nights later, at four o'clock in the morning, I all of a sudden woke up and had this feeling, "Go write this down for Judy McGuire," who was a teacher who teaches with my daughter. Judy had just lost her husband to cancer.

I went into my room and the words just kept coming as I wrote a prayer of comfort. It really shook me up, because . . . I never read poetry, don't like to read poetry. Still don't. I am a voracious reader, but I had never read poetry.

It really shook me up when I saw what I had written. I didn't have to edit it; it came word for word. This was the first poem I had ever written. Even in school, I hated writing poems. When I was in the fourth and fifth grades, we had to make up rhymes. I was terrible. I couldn't do it.

So I put away the poem I had just written. It frightened me.

I don't know if it was like when Job was being tested, like "Would you really follow through and be faithful?"

Following her NDE, Paige continues to write poetry. She signs her poems "Paige the Messenger."

Similarly, Darrell Pell was given a premonition a few days after his heart transplant:

> On Tuesday after the transplant, I called Alison from the hospital and told her that there were three things that I had to do—motorcycles, prisons, and children. I don't know why, but the Lord just told me "Motorcycles, prisons, and children."
>
> I got out of the hospital and a week later we drove by Milford Church of God and it said, "Christian Motorcyclists Association will be here on the last day of September." I told Alison, "This is where I need to be. I need to be in this church, this service, this night."

Darrell attended this service and joined the Christian Motorcyclists Association (see Chapter 2). He also began to counsel prisoners and to work with dying children as a chaplain at Scottish Rite Children's Hospital.

The most common type of precognitive knowledge was an awareness of the death or endangerment of a close friend or relative. Veronica, the nurse we met earlier, remembers vividly the night her mother died.

> I knew the time almost to the minute that my mother died. I was a little girl and I was living with my great-aunt, because my mother was in the hospital with cancer. I woke up in the middle of the night screaming, "She's dead. She's dead."
>
> My father was at the hospital with her. My aunt just tried to get me to go back to sleep. But I knew that she was dead. I found out the next morning that she had died.

Jon is a middle-aged liberal Christian who had a near-death experience during an auto accident while in high school. He was playing in a band at the time, and was driving a car pulling a trailer full of band equipment to an out-of-town gig. On a steep downgrade in the north Georgia mountains the car and trailer jackknifed, careened over a small retaining wall, and plummeted into a ravine, flipping over three times.

> The funny part of it is that my mother knew instantly when it happened. She knew something was wrong. And I had a girlfriend who I had been seeing for two or three years. She and I almost had an ESP connection. My girlfriend also knew something was wrong. She called my mother within two minutes after my mother knew something was wrong. They both felt that something had happened.
>
> By the time I called my mother, it was about three hours later. She was really agitated at that point and was glad to hear from me. She knew something had happened and wanted to know if I was alright.
>
> The distances would have been about 150 miles to my mother and 250 miles to my girlfriend.

This "ESP connection" between Jon and his girlfriend continued for many years after they had gone their separate ways.

> I had not seen, talked to, or heard from this girlfriend for six or seven years. I had not even thought about this girl. It was Thanksgiving day and at 7:30 in the morning I just had an uncontrollable urge to find her. I knew something was wrong.
>
> I called her mother and she said, "Jon! Thank God you called!"
>
> I said, "What's wrong with Marilyn?" and she began to relate to me that the night before, her husband had physically abused her and put her in the hospital out in Hawaii. I was sitting in South Carolina, thousands of miles away.

And Abigail, a conservative Christian, had a similar connection with her sister Marty. At the time of Marty's near-death experience, Abigail was asleep hundreds of miles away at college.

I suddenly woke up and knew that I had to get to Spartanburg, where my sister was. In a couple of minutes the phone rang and they said, "We don't know if she is going to make it." She had had an IUD and had gotten pregnant on it. In the fourth month, she miscarried. When she did, she had the toxic poisoning thing.

I knew that she was on the IUD, that she was going to lose the baby, and that she was going into the hospital. But as far as the things getting to the point of death, no way.

Among all near-death experiencers, precognitive experiences were reported by 55% of conservative Christians, 46% of liberal Christians, and 67% of God-believers. This compares to a report rate of 21% in the cardiac patient control group.[7]

Conclusions

Interest in psychic phenomena was definitely piqued in persons reporting a near-death experience, regardless of their religious beliefs. Moreover, "psychic experiences" such as visions and precognitive encounters were found more frequently among near-death experiencers than nonnear-death experiencers, but no significant difference was found in the occurrence of nonNDE-associated out-of-body experiences between these two groups.

The comments made by two conservative Christians about their out-of-body experiences are interesting. Both had put a negative spiritual spin on these encounters when they intentionally induced them, and they felt as if their efforts in this direction led them into Satan's path. When similar experiences occurred spontaneously, however, as during an NDE, no such condemnation was forthcoming.

Brooks Alexander, senior researcher for the Spiritual Counterfeits Project in Berkeley, California, explains further the danger of "psychic dabbling":

The fact is that no one knows how demonic beings operate in relation to psychic phenomena. Therefore it is impossible to say that "X" amount of psychic involvement will result in demonic contact. We do not know where the line is drawn between dabbling and demonism, or between curiosity and commitment, nor do we know how and when that line is crossed. It may be that the question of "how much" has less to do with it than we think. I would suggest that the neural and mental pattern set up by psychic involvement provides an *interface* with other forms of consciousness, which are extradimensional and demonic in nature. If that is the case, then psychic dabbling is a little like entering the cage of a man-eating tiger. You may or may not be eaten, depending in part on how hungry the tiger is. The significant point is that once you enter the cage, the initiative passes to the tiger.[8]

When the pre- and postNDE occurrence of out-of-body experiences, visions, and precognitions were compared, these psychic events did not appear to occur more frequently following the NDE—a finding that is not in line with other reports referenced at the beginning of this chapter. To me, this raises the question of whether an NDE truly leads to increased psychic abilities and sensitivities; whether an NDE increases one's awareness of an otherwise normal degree of psychic intuition; or whether having an NDE is a result, not a cause, of a predisposition to this behavior to begin with. The relationship of NDEs to psychic phenomena is very poorly understood.

Finally, Raymond Moody's warning at the beginning of this chapter is a real one. "Spiritualism with all its bizarre trappings" is a common outgrowth of the near-death experience. Along with the road to Omega, it is a path down which many NDE researchers and experiencers are led. And, as suggested by Brooks Alexander, it is a cage from which many will, unfortunately, not return.

In collusion with Moody, Kubler-Ross, and others ... Professor Ring and his previous colleagues of the IANDS group ... persist in the great white hope that only good experiences of unconditional love, without negative fears, will be found by each of us in the hereafter, thus spawning the philosophy that heaven's gates are open wide for everyone who dies.[1]

—MAURICE S. RAWLINGS, M.D.
TO HELL AND BACK, 1993

Nine

HELL:

Uncommon Near-Death

Fingers of ice were beginning to slowly form on the still-green needles of pine trees as I turned onto I–75 heading north out of Atlanta. I was on my way to meet Dr. Maurice Rawlings to discuss a difficult matter that had come between him and me over the preceding years. The driving conditions were hazardous that frosty February morning in 1994, so I had plenty of time to reflect as I inched along the icy interstate to Chattanooga.

I had briefly met Maurice backstage at a television program in 1978. His first book, *Beyond Death's Door*, had just been released, and we both had been flown in to discuss the near-death experience.

I thought at the time that this tall, lanky man with a deep voice and broad, easy smile would have fit right in on the streets of my hometown of Houston wearing a ten-gallon Stetson.

We each appeared on the program separately and kept our differences to ourselves. But those differences had already appeared in print. In a review of Maurice's book, I had examined the data presented in *Beyond Death's Door* and had concluded that it did not support the two main theses in the book.

First, Maurice claimed that "bad" near-death experiences would be found as frequently as "good" ones if persons were interviewed immediately after the near-death event. If interviewed later, near-death experiencers would report only "heavenly" experiences and would repress the "bad" or "hellish" ones. In support of this claim, Maurice offered only a few anecdotal cases. Most of his "hellish" NDEs were gathered from persons at a time distant from their resuscitation—a finding which simply contradicted his thesis that immediate interview is necessary to recover negative NDEs.

Second, Maurice presented the near-death experience as a literal trip to heaven or to hell. Consequently, Christian theology would require that Christians would have the pleasant or "heavenly" NDEs, and non-Christians the unpleasant or "hellish" ones. But other researchers, including myself, had found that Christian or non-Christian beliefs prior to an NDE did *not* influence the type of experience encountered.

Maurice's response to our findings was vociferous: Ring, Moody, myself and others were attempting to deny the reality of hell!

As I continued to creep up the frozen interstate to Chattanooga, I began to have second thoughts about having called this meeting. I was especially concerned about Maurice's reaction to my review of his latest book *To Hell and Back*, which I had sent him a couple of weeks before. I had called this meeting to discuss my review prior to submitting it to the publisher.

One case in particular bothered me the most.

In his 1978 book, *Beyond Death's Door*, Maurice presented the case of a Baptist Sunday school teacher. This teacher was said to have suffered three cardiac arrests, the first associated with a hellish NDE and the next two with heavenly experiences. He finally died from cancer of the large bowel.

With this case, Maurice found it "difficult to explain" how a "staunch Christian, the founder of a Sunday school, and a lifelong supporter of the church" had experienced a "hellish NDE"—an experience both the teacher (who identified himself as a "professing Christian") and Maurice were convinced was "the entrance to hell."

This same story then appeared in *To Hell and Back* 15 years later. This time, the man was said to have died during his third cardiac arrest, not sometime later from cancer, casting doubt on the reliability of medical details. More importantly, however, this once "staunch Christian" in *Beyond Death's Door* was now presented as one "who knew he was not the Christian he should have been" prior to his hellish NDE.

This critical modification of the story solved Maurice's original "problem" of how a supposed professing Christian could have had a hellish NDE—the man's Christian commitment had not been for real.

This posed new questions, however.

Had new information been obtained *after* publication of *Beyond Death's Door* to account for this major change in the story? Definitely not, since the man had been dead at the time of the first book's publication.

Furthermore, if this *now* non-Christian man went to hell, then why did he go to heaven shortly thereafter in his next NDE? The only plausible Christian explanation for this change in "afterlife destination" would be a religious conversion following his trip to hell and before his trip to heaven. This didn't make sense.

In *Beyond Death's Door*, Maurice knew of no such "transformation or dedication" and the teacher's heavenly NDE appeared "without apparent reason." In *To Hell and Back*, however, Maurice reported that "[s]ome sort of conversion resulted" from the hellish NDE, "and the second clinical death produced a wonderful, heavenly experience."

From my study of his books, I had concluded that Maurice had changed some of the key elements of this story and others to correspond with a preconceived agenda involving Christianity and the near-death experience.

I was deep in thought as I neared the southern edge of Chattanooga. The fog and ice had thickened, and I missed the turnoff to Maurice's house. In an effort to backtrack and reestablish my bearings, I got lost. With the help of a postman, I finally made it to the front of Maurice's house only a few minutes late.

I took a deep breath, opened the car door, and walked out into the icy mist. I had no idea how Maurice would receive my criticism, and I braced for the worst.

My fears melted as Mrs. Rawlings graciously greeted me at the front door and ushered me into a sprawling ranch-style house. A much-welcomed hot cup of coffee was immediately thrust into my hand.

Maurice quickly appeared. We shook hands and retired to his study.

After exchanging a few idle comments about the weather, Maurice began first. He apologized for having implicated me in a "collusion" to suppress a belief in hell. In the case of the Baptist Sunday school teacher, he agreed that there were inaccuracies in this report, but countered that he had been more interested in a correct Christian message than an accurate research report. In retrospect, as he put it, "it would have been better to have just rubber-stamped the experiences from one book to the next and avoided the appearance of fish stories." Maurice still was convinced, however, that the hellish NDE would be recalled, except in rare cases, only immediately following a resuscitation.

At the end of our meeting, I encouraged him to write a response to my review. He then volunteered the idea of writing an addendum to future editions of *To Hell and Back,* correcting some of his errors.

After lunch in a local restaurant, we parted friends.

The following year, we met again—this time as speakers at the IANDS International Meeting in San Antonio.

And our friendship has continued.

My review of *To Hell and Back* was published in the spring of 1996 in the *Journal of Near-Death Studies.* Maurice did not write a response. The addendum to *To Hell and Back,* to my knowledge, has not yet appeared.

Despite the inaccuracies in Maurice's work, he still is credited with alerting us to the "frightening" or "negative" near-death experience. In followup, Bruce Greyson and Nancy Bush began collecting reports of this type of NDE in 1982. Ten years later, they had collected only 50 cases, which they presented in the medical journal *Psychiatry*. These hellish NDEs conformed to one of three patterns.

The first pattern had the features of a typical NDE—separation from body, moving through a tunnel, seeing a light, et cetera—but the experience was terrifying, not comforting. "Loss of ego control" was the reason proposed for this paradoxical response.

The second pattern was labeled "eternal nothingness" and included "eternal emptiness, an experience of being mocked, and a sense of all of life being an illusion . . . [which] leave the individual with a pervasive sense of emptiness and fatalistic despair after the event."[2]

The third and final pattern was the "'hellish' experience characterized by archetypal imagery, sounds of torment, and sometimes demonic beings."

Brief mention was made of the religious backgrounds of nine experiencers in the report—"no religious background" in three; "raised as a Protestant, Congregationalist, and Presbyterian" in three; one a "daughter of Unitarian ministers"; one whose "family attended Dutch Reformed Church," and one Jew. In other words, there appeared to be no obvious relationship between religion and "hell."

Would I find the same trend in The Atlanta Study?

Trips to "Hell"

At the beginning of my study, I knew finding hellish NDEs would be difficult. In my first study I had interviewed 71 consecutive near-death experiencers, some immediately following their near-death event, and had not found one frightening experience. Moreover, George Gallup had found in a nationwide survey that only 1% of near-death experiencers reported a sense of hell or torment; and it had taken Greyson and Bush 10 years to collect 50 cases.

In The Atlanta Study, however, I was able to locate two cases of experiences with "hell." Jake, the 40-year-old wheelchair-bound veteran first introduced in Chapter 6, had attempted suicide 13 years before. Deeply depressed, he explained,

> I had gone up to the mountains to die. I took 20 or 30 Quaaludes and several cans of beer. It was a suicide attempt.
>
> I was all alone and passed out. I was in a place like hell. It was like a valley and the earth had been scorched. There were demons like in a Bosch painting. There was vapor rising from the ground like steam. The sky was overcast with grayish clouds.
>
> I felt awful—depressed and miserable. Unbearable. I didn't have my body anymore. This was worse than anything I ever experienced before.
>
> The demons were giving me a bad time, making fun of me and kicking me. I was falling down a lot.
>
> There was chain lightning in the background and God spoke to me, not in a voice but like a voice saying, "You could have had anything you wanted—you threw it away." During this time, the sky would light up like heat lightning when God spoke.
>
> I thought to myself that I could have been anything that I wanted to be. I had just destroyed it.
>
> I remember begging. I threw myself to my knees and prayed, "Forgive me. I want to live. God, please help me."
>
> All of a sudden, I begged real hard and I came to throwing up the Quaaludes.
>
> I think that my spirit left my body. I was out of my body and went to a waiting room. This was real, not a nightmare.
>
> I have a deep belief in God and that he loved me and was looking over me.

The second case of hell was reported by Beau, a retired grocery store owner, who had collapsed at home on the floor of his kitchen while opening a can of soup. Hearing the fall, his wife ran in from the living room and tried to revive him. Their son then arrived and continued CPR while she called 911. Beau was still in ventricular fibrillation when the EMTs arrived. One shock from the defibrillator restored normal rhythm, but it would be two weeks before Beau regained consciousness due to severe hypoxic brain damage. He would later recall a near-death experience in which he initially went to hell and then was transported to heaven.

I left this world. I can remember just a spirit. I went to hell. Or I called it hell cause it was hot. I thought that was my place.

I ran into my brother-in-law. I talked to him. He seemed to be working. He was a good man except when liquor got hold of him, and then he was just rough and mean. This man had been dead for about four or five years. Hell was hot, uncomfortable. Seemed like it was lower down.

Along came my guide or guardian angels. I knew some of them. Some of them were family friends. One was my uncle, another was my wife's uncle, and a third was my father's good friend. They were in spirit form somehow.

These guardian angels—I may be confused here, I don't know—they said that there had been a mistake made, that I was going to move up. I can't understand that now, doc, because I don't believe they make mistakes.

The guardian angels looked like clouds, but I communicated with them, I talked to them. I knew who they were. I don't remember seeing a light at the end of a tunnel.

The guardian angel told me to come on, we were moving. I ran into my father. I talked to him. I had the feeling that he was happy and that he was working. We moved on, seemed to be moving up now. I seemed to be floating over on my grandfather's place. It just seemed like in my mind I could look down and see the cleared fields, and the bridge where the creek was at. We were just floating in a cloud or something above.

I looked out there and there was a line of people. They were dressed in purple robes with the prettiest gold glitter on the chest part. I got to meeting these people, to shaking hands with them. They were introducing themselves. They were all my relatives, the way I remember them. And I began to be happy.

That was one of the most beautiful sights I ever seen, all those purple robes.

About this time I didn't get to meet them all because the guardian angel told me that I had to go back. I remember that I didn't want to come back. It seemed real to me. I was happy, very happy.

I don't know whether I questioned him or not. He told me that I had to go back for my grandchildren and my children. That's the way I remember it.

As I was coming back, they told me several things. They told me that I would eventually forget this except for two things: there was a heaven and there was a hell. And that the Golden Rule will get a person to heaven.

They told me that I could tell my experience to my relatives and to my friends who would believe it. They said that I would not be a preacher or a teacher. They said I would be a person, an average Christian.

Then I woke up in what seemed like a dark hallway, mighty dark and dreary, in the hospital. For a while, all I wanted to do was to tell my experience. I called my preacher. I just felt like I had to tell him.

Why all of this happened to me, I don't know. I've been a fairly good man, but not an outstanding Christian. A backslider. But I always tried to treat people right. I was in the grocery business for 40 years. I met a lot of people and I always tried to be honest.

I know I met my brother-in-law. I know I met my daddy. I know there is a hell. And I know there is a heaven.

Both of these hellish NDEs fit into Greyson's and Bush's third pattern of hellish imagery and demonic beings.

Jake had been raised in the Catholic church, but had left the church long before his NDE. As mentioned earlier, he had two of the lowest scores in The Atlanta Study on his Spiritual Beliefs Questionnaire and Hoge's scale—a 3.5 and a 14 respectively. His NDE occurred while attempting suicide.

The association of suicide attempts with hellish NDEs has been noted before. Maurice Rawlings has written: "I have never seen any good case result from attempted suicide.... All attempted self-euthanasias have been uniformly negative, not positive."[3] Also, two of the three pattern-three examples of NDE hell in Greyson and Bush's *Psychiatry* article occurred during suicide attempts.

In The Atlanta Study, however, two cases of suicide-induced NDEs other than Jake's were not hellish in nature. Nevertheless, suicide attempts overall may be more frequently associated with a hellish NDE, and a possible reason for this will be explored in the final chapter.

Beau had been raised Southern Baptist, rarely attended church, and likewise scored low on the two questionnaires—a 5.5 and a 20. This near-death experience appeared to have led him away from Baptist doctrine. "Guardian angels" such as described by Beau were frequently reported in the Greyson and Bush series as well. It was Beau's impression that he initially ended up in hell because of a mistake made by these angels. This confused him, since he believed that angels don't make mistakes.

In fact, angels *do* make mistakes, for God "charges his angels with error" (Job 4:18). Bible commentator Matthew Henry explains:

> If the world were left to the government of the angels, and they were trusted with the sole management of affairs, they would take false steps, and everything would not be done for the best, as now it is. Angels are intelligences, but finite ones.[4]

But I'm getting ahead of myself. Before we consider the issue of angels, let us take one more stroll down the halls of science and medicine.

In the latter part of the twentieth century, we have such a need to be unique, to be special, to be different. You know the thing that unifies so many of these people—they are so narcissistic. It's "Look at me. I saw God. I saw Jesus. I am different." ... Since those experiences are explainable on a perfectly straightforward biological basis, we don't have to invoke supernatural events to explain them.

—Sherwin B. Nuland, M.D.
Professor of Surgery, Yale University
As quoted on NBC's Dateline,
August 14, 1996

Ten

SCIENTIFIC EXPLANATIONS:

Nailing Jell-O to the Wall

When I had first been introduced to Raymond Moody's book *Life After Life*, in 1976, I remember thinking that, for someone with a Ph.D. and M.D. behind his name, Moody was horribly *unscientific*. His book was based on interviews with "some 50 persons" whom he haphazardly identified as "a woman," "a man," "a young informant," and "several persons" who had survived "a severe illness," "a wreck," "death," and so forth. No protocols had been followed, no data or tables presented, no medical details given.

Despite these scientific deficiencies, *Life After Life* became an international bestseller. The book captured my imagination and led me into my own study of the phenomenon. But I refused to leave science behind. I was convinced that the near-death experience, if properly studied, could be reduced to a simple scientific explanation.

Five years and 116 interviews later, I found that I was wrong. No explanation had been found.

Since my first study conducted nearly two decades ago, science has progressed. New research has been conducted, new papers have been written, and new explanations have appeared. Honoring these new developments, I reopen the question, "Can science explain the near-death experience?"

Flatliners

In the 1990 movie *Flatliners*, four medical students induce cardiac arrest in each other in an attempt to encounter a near-death experience. While the circumstances of this movie are clearly fictional, experiments such as these have actually been carried out.

Physicians at the University of California School of Medicine in San Francisco deliberately precipitated 22 episodes of cardiac arrest in 14 patients to test the function of their automatic implantable cardioverter defibrillator.[1] These defibrillators are pocket-sized devices (similar to pacemakers) that are surgically implanted and connected to the heart with wire leads. They detect the onset of ventricular tachycardia or fibrillation and then automatically deliver an electrical shock to the heart to correct the rhythm. After implantation, they are tested by inducing cardiac arrest while the patient is under anesthesia. But this California study is unique in that the patients were fully awake at the time of the cardiac arrest, and their psychological experiences were evaluated along with electrocardiographic, EEG, and video recordings.

Consciousness was lost nine to 21 seconds after stoppage of the heart. Prior to loss of consciousness, the patients felt "distant, dazed, and as if they were fading out." After regaining consciousness five to 150 seconds later, they remained confused for up to 30 seconds. Unlike the movie *Flatliners*, however, no near-death experiences were reported by these University of California researchers.

Death has also been experimentally approached using a specially designed inflatable cuff placed around the lower third of the necks of 137 volunteers.[2] The cuff was inflated to 600 millimeters of mercury (normal mean blood pressure is 100 millimeters of mercury) in one-eighth of a second, causing complete arrest of the cerebral circulation. It was kept inflated for up to 100 seconds with the subjects connected to EEGs and other physiological monitoring devices.

After five or six seconds of cuff inflation and cerebral anoxia, subjects' eyes suddenly fixed in the midline. Consciousness was lost one-half to one second later. Immediately before loss of consciousness, many subjects experienced rapid narrowing of the fields of vision, blurring of vision, with the field of vision becoming gray, and finally, complete loss of vision. A number of subjects stated that they were unable to see but could still hear and were conscious. Occasionally subjects reported that they experienced positive or negative scotomas, such as light or dark streaks or spots or twinkling lights progressing inward from the periphery of the visual field.[3]

During longer periods of cervical occlusion, severe convulsions with "marked cyanosis, involuntary urination and defecation, bradycardia [slowed heart beat], dilatation of the pupils and changes in reflexes were recorded."[4] Amazingly, no permanent ill effects were reported. Nothing resembling a near-death experience—such as a tunnel; a bright, all-encompassing light; spirit figures; et cetera—were mentioned.

Finally, 1,000 air force pilots were taken to the brink with extreme degrees of head to foot acceleration in a human centrifuge.[5] Under these conditions, the heart can no longer supply blood to the brain, creating "gravitational loss of consciousness" or G-LOC. If the centrifuge is not immediately stopped at this point, death results.

During the first six seconds of gravitational stress, subjects report tunnel vision with contraction of the visual field from the periphery inward. Blackout, or complete loss of vision, occurs next, and then unconsciousness. During the more severe episodes of G-LOC, when the insult to the brain was the greatest, "dreamlets," or short dream interludes, occurred in some subjects.

The content of these dreamlets fit two patterns.[6] Some subjects felt as if they were "in enclosed spaces such as a closet or small room." These interludes were associated with "confusion, anxiety, frustration, [or] a sense of 'paralysis'." Other interludes "were generally set in open areas during daylight and were colorful." These were associated with feeling "generally happy (euphoric) [or] relaxed." Common to both types was the incorporation of ongoing physical events into dream content.

For instance, some subjects dreamed they were riding in "bumper cars" at an amusement park while, at the same time, their heads were rhythmically jerking against the seat in the centrifuge. Another person integrated the jiggling of his arms in the centrifuge into a dreamlet of fishing and pulling back on a fishing rod several times to set the hook. These dreamlets met all the characteristic features of dreams, including "emotional intensity, detailed sensory imagery, illogical content and organization, uncritical acceptance, and difficulty in remembering once it is over."[7]

Typical near-death experiences were not reported during G-LOC, leading the author, Dr. James Whinnery, to conclude that symptoms "unique to the NDE" are beyond the scope of this type of experimentation and require longer forays into the process of dying.

"Dying Brain" Theories

The human brain is critically dependent on a rich supply of oxygen and nutrients. Impairment of this supply, even for only a few seconds, may lead to a myriad of electrical and biochemical events.

Seizures are caused by abnormal electrical discharges within the brain and may occur immediately prior to death. They were found, at times, in the *Flatliners*-like experiments. Seizures in the temporal lobes of the brain may cause visual hallucinations of complex geometric shapes; distortions of color, time, and space; memory flashbacks; feelings of *deja vu;* and (rarely) feeling "out of the body." These seizures are thought by some researchers to cause the near-death experience. Endorphins and hypoxia (lack of oxygen) have both been proposed as triggers for temporal lobe seizures in the dying brain.

Endorphins are morphine-like substances synthesized and released by the brain under conditions of stress such as anxiety, fear, or pain. These brain chemicals are known to produce a state of painlessness and calm in the face of life-threatening danger.

This action was recently illustrated to me by one of my patients. This woman described being brutally attacked late one night at an automatic teller machine. Surprised from behind, she felt complete terror and panic. Her assailant dragged her into a nearby ditch and began repeatedly stabbing her in the face and chest. At one point her pain and fear vanished, and an overwhelming feeling of calm took over. Her body went limp, but she remained conscious. Thinking that she had died, her attacker dropped her to the ground and fled. Her sudden physical and mental change in the face of life-threatening danger resulted almost certainly from the release of endorphins, which in turn may have saved her life.

Whether endorphins cause seizures, however, is unclear. In a recent review of the latest research on endorphins published in the *International Journal of Clinical Pharmacology, Therapy and Toxicology*, the authors conclude that both pro- and anticonvulsant effects have been reported, thus making it "difficult to draw conclusions about the pathophysiological role of endogenous opioid peptides [i.e., endorphins] in epilepsy."[8] The authors even suggested that endorphins may be effective in treating, not causing, temporal lobe seizures.

On the other hand, hypoxia has been shown to increase the brain's susceptibility to seizures, including seizures of the temporal lobe.

Dr. Michael Persinger, Professor of Neuroscience and Psychology at Laurentian University in Canada, has mimicked temporal lobe seizure phenomena by electrical stimulation of the brain. These induced experiences were "fragmented and variable, whereas in NDEs these sensations are integrated and focused within a brief period."[9]

This loss of mental integration is a key feature that separates seizure phenomena from the near-death experience. Dr. Denis Williams found in a massive study of 2,000 epileptic patients that seizures do not cause spontaneous primary cognition, since cognition is purely an integrative function. The epileptic experience can include hallucinations of sight, sound, smell and even hallucinations of emotion and mood, but it does not cause hallucinations of thought.[10]

But in the near-death experience, thought is often clear and complex. Listen to Greg, for instance, describe his thinking during his NDE:

> I am a computer analyst. I grew up with computers.... As God is my witness, I was out of my body and up by the corner ceiling of the hospital room looking down on the situation. I was trying to figure out how I could do that—be up there and be down there at the same time.... I thought to myself, *Now, this is strange.* But there was no alarm. I was completely cool.
>
> Just about that time I got to thinking on that pretty good, suddenly I found myself in the tunnel of light.... My analytical background told me that this was so interesting. I tried to drink in the sights as long as I could.... Still, my mind was so sharp that I was joking with myself, even at that time ... I thought I was in heaven. I saw these white images moving in that diffused white light and I said to myself, "Wow. At least I came to the right place," because I thought they were angels....
>
> This is the interesting part of all this. I knew the seriousness of the situation, and I knew I was into some realm that I had never been in before. I knew I was on my way to something. I didn't know exactly what, but I knew enough from my religious teachings to call on the Lord Jesus Christ.
>
> I was able to think rationally, coolly, and make decisions while my body was elsewhere and my soul was in the hands of God.

Dr. Williams also found in his comprehensive study of 2,000 epileptics that only 1 in 20 patients feels emotion during a seizure. When present, these emotions were fear, depression, or displeasure 91% of the time. With a near-death experience, however, 87% of Atlanta Study subjects felt "incredible peace or painlessness," 11% "relief or calm," and only 2% "neither." Emotions during the NDE, moreover, were "incredible joy" 62% of the time, "happiness" in 21% of the cases, and "neither" in only 17%.

In the 9% of Williams' seizure patients reporting a pleasurable emotion, the emotion was *always* associated with a visceral or bodily sensation such as "goose skin," "a disturbance of breathing," "a pleasant warm sinking feeling in abdomen," "heart pounds," or "a pleasant but indescribable taste in my mouth." These physical symptoms are virtually never a component of an NDE.

Dr. Ernst Rodin, Medical Director of the Epilepsy Center of Michigan and Professor of Neurology at Wayne State University, puts the issue in perspective:

> The hallmarks and nuclear components of NDEs are a sensation of peace or even bliss, the knowledge of having died, and, as a result, being no longer limited by the physical body. In spite of having seen hundreds of patients with temporal lobe seizures during three decades of professional life, I have never come across that symptomatology as part of a seizure.[11]

Thus, the "dying brain hypothesis," which attempts to explain the NDE on the basis of endorphins, hypoxia, and temporal lobe seizures, cannot adequately account for the near-death experience. To do so would be like confusing bronchitis and pneumonia—there may be similarities, but the trained medical observer knows that they are fundamentally different conditions with different symptoms and methods of treatment.

"Visual" Perception During the Out-of-Body Experience

During the out-of-body or autoscopic portion of the near-death experience, the dying person feels as if he floats out of his physical body and looks down. "Autoscopic" is a word meaning "self-visualization."

In my first book, I was able to verify some of the details of these visual, out-of-body perceptions, raising the possibility that "paranormal" perception may have actually occurred. Since this study—over 15 years ago—little headway has been made in our understanding of this fascinating phenomenon. My work remains "the only evidence from systematic research in the field of near-death studies that suggests near-death experiencers can sometimes report visual perceptions that are physically impossible and not otherwise explicable by conventional means."[12]

Nevertheless, the discussion continues.

One popular theory is that these out-of-body experiences are hallucinations reconstructed from visual and auditory perceptions *prior* to loss of consciousness. In support of this theory is the research reported in Chapter 4 which shows that in fact consciousness is not lost for several seconds after the onset of a cardiac arrest. When recollections from the semiconscious period and from the NDE are compared, however, clear differences are described.

Recall, for example, Brent and Greg from Chapter 4. Each of these men described events which occurred while semiconscious and "in the body." Suddenly, a well-defined out-of-body experience began that was clearly different from "in the body" perceptions. I noted this as a passage from "terror" to "tranquillity"—a passage that corresponds to the experimentally-determined onset of unconsciousness nine to 21 seconds after the beginning of the arrest.

Moreover, in *Recollections*, I presented several details from these autoscopic NDEs which had been of objects or events out of physical view of the arrested patient and not audibly discussed by others present at the arrest. When these recollections were of medical procedures, the degree of accuracy of the recalled procedures was much greater than that found in the common knowledge of hospital-savvy cardiac patients. These findings support the contention that the autoscopic NDE is not a reconstructed hallucination.

Other researchers have wondered why the autoscopic NDE is always described as looking down from an elevated, bird's-eye viewpoint. Psychologist Susan Blackmore has proposed that during an NDE, "the normal model of reality breaks down and the system tries to get back to normal by building a new model from memory and imagination. If this model is from a bird's-eye view, then an out-of-body experience takes place."[13]

Dr. William Serdahely examined Blackmore's hypothesis. He classified memory as either "observer memory," in which one recalls seeing or observing oneself from the outside as in an out-of-body experience, or "field memory," in which the recollection is of oneself looking out from the physical body. Blackmore posits that the out-of-body experience is constructed from "memory and imagination." Since memory and imagination are constructed from everyday experience, and everyday experience is most commonly registered in the "field memory" mode, then, according to Blackmore's theory, the autoscopic portion of the NDE should frequently be "nonautoscopic"—that is, an in-the-body or "field memory" experience, and not exclusively the "observer memory" phenomenon that it is. Accordingly, Serdahely concludes that the autoscopic NDE is *not* fashioned from one's memory and imagination, but is most likely an *actual experience*.

Also crucial to Blackmore's theory is her prediction that "NDErs who have out-of-body experiences as part of their experience should be those who use bird's-eye views more in imagination and dreaming." I tested this prediction. When 40 near-death experiencers were asked whether they dreamed as "participants" (i.e., field memory) or as "observers" (i.e., observer memory), 73% claimed to be participants in their dreams. No difference was found, moreover, between the dreaming modes of near-death experiencers with (21 persons) and without (19 persons) an autoscopic near-death experience.

How, then, do these theories hold up during an actual near-death experience in a scientific laboratory?

Pam's Near-Death Experience

Pam Reynolds, whom we first met in Chapter 3, reported the deepest near-death experience of The Atlanta Study at a time when her brain and body were extensively instrumented and monitored.

Could Pam's NDE have resulted from a temporal lobe seizure? Clinically, such seizures are detected by abnormal brain-wave patterns on an EEG. Her brain-wave activity was continuously monitored, and no seizure phenomena were reported. Furthermore, her surgeon, Dr. Robert Spetzler, told me that he "has never known of someone having a temporal lobe seizure during this procedure." He felt it would be "extremely unlikely" that such a seizure would occur since Pam's brain had been silenced with massive amounts of "barbiturate protection."

Could Pam have heard the intraoperative conversation and then used this to reconstruct an out-of-body experience? At the beginning of the procedure, molded ear speakers were placed in each ear as a test for auditory and brain-stem reflexes. These speakers occlude the ear canals and altogether eliminate the possibility of physical hearing. Despite this, she reports having heard, during her out-of-body experience, "something about my veins and arteries being very small. I believe it was a female voice and that it was Dr. Murray, but I'm not sure. She was the cardiologist [*sic*]. I remember thinking that I should have told her about that."

Dr. Murray was the female cardiovascular surgeon in the case. In her operative report, she had dictated in her section on "Findings at the time of surgery" that the right femoral artery and vein were exposed, and the right common femoral artery was quite small, approximating the size of a normal saphenous vein bypass. Due to its 4-mm size, it would not accept a #18 arterial cannula. It was decided that, in order to achieve appropriate flows for bypass, bilateral groin cannulation would be necessary. This was discussed with Neurosurgery, as it would affect angio access postoperatively for arteriography.

From this evidence, we can conclude that the conversation actually occurred and that its content was accurately recalled. Also, the timing of this conversation with the reported occurrence of the out-of-body experience was found to be precise.

Pam stated that she did not hear or perceive anything prior to her out-of-body experience, and that this experience began with hearing the bone saw. At this point in the operation, she had been under anesthesia for about 90 minutes. If the conversation she claims to have heard had occurred prior to or after this point in the surgery, then this recollection would not correspond to her out-of-body experience and would rule against the accuracy of Pam's story.

Dr. Spetzler dictated into his operative report that "simultaneous with the opening of the craniotomy, Dr. Murray performed bilateral femoral cut-downs for cannulation for cardiac bypass." "Craniotomy" means cutting open the skull with the bone saw. Dr. Murray would have conversed about the size of Pam's vessels at the time she was performing the cut-downs. Thus, the "opening [or beginning] of the craniotomy" using the bone saw was simultaneous with the conversation about Pam's small blood vessels—and, as it turns out, with her out-of-body experience. This correspondence of Pam's recollections from an out-of-body experience with the correct bit of intraoperative conversation during a six-hour operative procedure is certainly intriguing evidence in support of Pam's story.

But was Pam's *visual* recollection from her out-of-body experience accurate?

When I first interviewed Pam on November 11, 1994, I was unfamiliar with the neurosurgical instruments used in this procedure. As a matter of routine, however, I ask for details recalled from an out-of-body experience. This point in my interview with Pam is transcribed below:

> Sabom: Did you see any specifics in the operating room during your experience?
>
> Pam: I remember seeing several things in the operating room when I was looking down.... I remember the heart-lung machine. I didn't like the respirator. But there were so many of them in different places and different points in the body. I remember a lot of tools and instruments that I did not readily recognize.
>
> Sabom: Were there any details that you had not seen before?
>
> Pam: The saw thing that I hated the sound of looked like an electric toothbrush and it had a dent in it, a groove at the top where the saw appeared to go into the handle, but it didn't.... And the saw had interchangeable blades, too, but these blades were in what looked like a socket wrench case.... I heard the saw crank up. I didn't see them use it on my head, but I think I heard it being used on something. It was humming at a relatively high pitch and then all of a sudden it went *Brrrrrrrrrr!* like that.

When I heard Pam's description of the bone saw that Dr. Spetzler used to open her skull, I cringed. An "electric toothbrush" with "interchangeable blades"? No way!

I filed the interview tape and did not listen to it for over a year while my research continued.

In March 1996, I transcribed Pam's tape and began to research the documentation of her story. I phoned the Midas

Rex Company in Fort Worth, Texas, and they sent me a student's user manual with pictures of the bone saw used by Dr. Spetzler. I was shocked with the accuracy of Pam's description of the saw as an "electric toothbrush" with "interchangeable blades" (See Figure 3) and with a "socket wrench case" in which this equipment is kept (See Figure 4).

But Pam's description of the bone saw having a "groove at the top where the saw appeared to go into the handle" was a bit puzzling. If viewed from the side (see Figure 5), the end of the bone saw has an overhanging edge that looks somewhat like a groove. However, it was not located "where the saw appeared to go into the handle" but at the other end.

Why had this apparent discrepancy arisen in Pam's description? Of course, the first explanation is that she did not "see" the saw at all, but was describing it from her own best guess of what it would look and sound like. The details that apparently correlated accurately with the saw would then have been merely coincidental. Another possible explanation is that she actually did "see" the saw

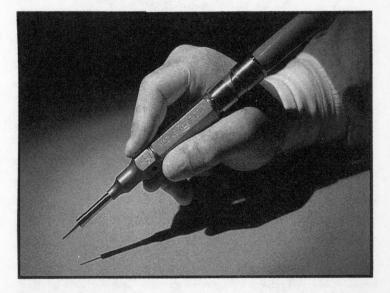

Figure 3: The Midas Rex bone saw in the hand of a surgeon.

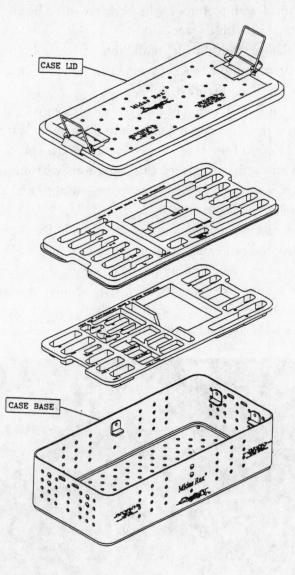

Figure 4: Midas Rex Neurosurgery Instrument Case and Trays which Pam described as a "socket wrench case."

from a distance, giving a fairly accurate description of the saw, "interchangeable blades," and case they were stored in, but was not able to precisely "see" the tip of the saw. This saw is quite small and, when being moved around in use, may be very difficult to see accurately.

Further exploration of Pam's case continues to raise the same questions: If we accept what she "saw" or "heard" as being accurate, then could she have been told about it either before or after the surgery to allow for the correct description, could she have somehow known about it from her own knowledge, or could it have been just coincidence? These are all legitimate questions that continue to becloud the claim of the near-

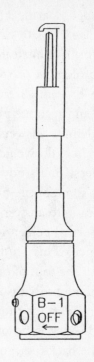

Figure 5: Drawing of the B-1 bone saw "blade" (actual size) used in Pam's surgery. This attachment to the saw was used instead of the one shown in Figure 3.

death experiencer that "I saw it from the ceiling." For some, evidence arising from cases such as Pam's will continue to suggest some type of out-of-body experience occurring when death is imminent. For others, the inexactness which arises in the evaluation of these cases will be reason enough to dismiss them as dreams, hallucinations, or fantasies.

Nailing Jell-O to the Wall

This brief walk with the near-death experience through the halls of science has left us standing pretty much where we were two decades ago. Daring *Flatliner*-like experiments taking volunteers to the edge of death have not reproduced the near-death experience. Nor have intricate theories involving complex biochemical and neurological processes explained the experience. And the promise of Pam's near-perfect laboratory conditions, with its detailed and accurate physiological data, gives us tantalizing clues, but no definite answers.

So where do we go from here?

At least one study is underway at the present time which bypasses some of the problems inherent in relying on anecdotal, clinical cases to answer the question of whether or not some sort of paranormal perception actually occurs during an out-of-body experience. This study employs randomly numbered targets placed on the tops of operating room and emergency room lights and equipment that can be visualized only from an out-of-body position next to the ceiling. So far, no "hits" have been reported—that is, no one has yet had an out-of-body experience and come back to accurately report the number sequence of the targets. If such a "hit" is ever documented, however, many of the pitfalls of the type of verification work I did with Pam and with others in my first book will be avoided.

At this juncture, I believe the near-death experience will continue to elude its capture and elucidation within the scientific laboratory. After completion of my first study, in the closing chapter of *Recollections of Death,* I referred to Wilder Penfield, the renowned neurosurgeon who spent a lifetime studying the human brain. In what Penfield termed "a final examination of the evidence" shortly before his death in April 1976, he expressed surprise at discovering that the mind, spirit, or soul of a person could not be reduced to the workings of the physical brain, but that the "mind has energy. . . . different from that of neuronal potentials that travel the axone pathways."[14]

In my research with the near-death experience, I, like Penfield, have discovered the footprints of a nonphysical "energy" at play—an energy deeply intertwined with a faith that Sir William Osler has likened to "an unfailing stream of energy;" and with prayer that Alexis Carrell has called the "most powerful" form of this energy. I have found that this energy powerfully impacts the practice of medicine—a practice which Francis Peabody believed laid, in part, "outside the realm of any science."

I have been challenged by others, such as Sherwin Nuland, who assert that NDEs are explainable on a "perfectly straightforward biological basis," and that the near-death experiencers' claim of seeing God or Jesus arises from their "narcissistic" desire to be unique. We have seen, however, that Nuland's biologic explanation, if present at all, is anything but straightforward and simple. But what about the rest of Nuland's assertion? Have near-death experiencers seen God? Have they seen Jesus?

As a Christian, a physician, and a near-death experience researcher, I now turn to a consideration of Who ties it all together.

I believe that all NDEs cannot be explained away on the basis of natural factors, even if some NDEs are susceptible to merely physical explanations.... The near-death experience proves to be a challenge to the materialism of modern science, just as it challenges those who are spiritually inclined to interpret its meaning properly.[1]

—DOUG GROOTHUIS, PH.D.
ASSISTANT PROFESSOR OF PHILOSOPHY
OF RELIGION AND ETHICS, DENVER SEMINARY
1995

Eleven

CONCLUSIONS:

The Bible and the Near-Death Experience

Shortly after *Recollections of Death* was published in January 1982, I got a call from a minister serving a large church in central Georgia. He had read my book and was excited about my findings. We talked for a while, and then came the shocker: He wanted *me* to preach a sermon on Easter Sunday!

Having absolutely no experience in the pulpit, I hastily declined.

After I hung up, I began to wonder, *What had I written in my book that made him request a sermon on the morning celebrating the resurrection of Jesus Christ?* I had identified myself in the book as a member of a Methodist Sunday school class and had suggested that the NDE may involve God. Throughout the book, however, I had made no effort to point the reader either toward or away from a belief in Jesus Christ. It didn't seem to me that the book implied any qualifications to preach an Easter sermon.

But I had to admit, my work had touched on a subject dear to the hearts of all Christians: life after death. And, as I was to learn in the years to come, the association of the NDE with this theological issue would generate major squabbles—squabbles in which, I'm afraid, I am about to become a part.

Before entering the fray, however, let me confide a few personal notes. Since *Recollections of Death*, my love of Scripture has grown, my walk with the Lord has deepened, and I have benefited from the teaching and encouragement of several Christian leaders in the Atlanta area. In 1993 I joined the Presbyterian

Church in America—a conservative Christian denomination—
and was ordained an elder shortly before writing this book.

Armed with a more profound understanding of the Christian
faith and deeper spiritual maturity, I now reconsider the near-
death experience and extend the discussion to include the One
whom I had left out before—Jesus Christ.

The Bible as My Guide

The names "Jesus" and "Christ" are not newcomers to books on
the near-death experience. Raymond Moody dedicated *Life After
Life* to "George Ritchie, M.D. and, through him, to the One
whom he suggested." Raymond later identified "the One" as
"Christ." Chuck Flynn dedicated *After the Beyond* to "Jesus, the
Universal Christ." Betty Eadie dedicated *Embraced by the Light* to
"The Light, my Lord and Savior Jesus Christ." And so on.

But who exactly is this "Jesus Christ"?

Most NDE authors would probably agree with Phyllis Atwater, who writes in *Coming Back to Life* that

> Jesus rarely if ever accepted "Messiah" as applicable to him dur-
> ing his lifetime, preferring instead the title, "Son of Man." Long
> after his crucifixion, it was the Western mind which named
> Jesus "The Christ" and established his identity as the Son of
> God. Since then, "Christ" has also come to symbolize Christ
> Consciousness or Christ Mind, which, it is said, anyone can
> possess.[2]

Despite assertions such as these, there is clear evidence in the
Bible that Jesus accepted the title of "Messiah." The woman at
the Samaritan well, for example, said, "I know that Messiah
(called Christ) is coming. When he comes, he will explain everything to us." Then Jesus declared, "I who speak to you am he"
(John 4:25–26).

Also, the title "Son of Man" is an Old Testament reference to
Jesus, the one "given dominion, glory and a kingdom, that all the

peoples, nations, and *men of every* language might serve Him" (Dan. 7:14 NASB). The "Son of Man" is unmistakably identified as the "Son of God" (John 5:24–27) by Jesus himself.

When Jesus asked his disciples who they thought he was, Simon Peter responded, "You are the Christ, the Son of the living God" (Matt. 16:16), a reply which Jesus endorsed by blessing Peter. Jesus and his disciples conspired, early in their ministry, to conceal Jesus' identity as the Christ (Matt. 16:20). After Jesus had preached throughout Israel and his work and ministry had become well known, however, his identity as the Christ was one he was willing to die for. When Jesus was asked by the religious leaders: "Are you the Christ, the Son of the Blessed One?" (Mark 14:61) he replied, "I am" (v. 62). This led immediately to his condemnation, ridicule, and abuse, and in fact the death sentence (vv. 64–65). Clearly, Jesus held that his identity as the Christ and the Son of God was sufficiently important for him to maintain it in the face of overwhelming opposition and personal loss. To dispute the traditional identity of Jesus as the Christ and the Son of God is not to argue with church teachers years after his crucifixion, but to contradict Jesus' own teaching.

In the discussion that follows, the above biblical definition of Jesus Christ will be used rather than recent inventions such as "the Christ Mind" and the like. In addition, the NDE will be evaluated in light of biblical evidence, not the reverse. NDE data will not be used as a substitute for or an addition to biblical truth. Nor will the Bible be made to speak where, in reality, it is silent. As a scientist, I strive to avoid jumping to conclusions, and I take the facts and deal with them honestly without adding my own spin to them. I believe that the Bible deserves the same reasonable treatment. According to the Bible, some mysteries of God are not meant for man to know (Deut. 29:29; Rom. 11:33; 1 Cor. 13:12). As John Calvin, the famed sixteenth-century Geneva lawyer, so aptly instructed, "Of those things which it is neither given nor lawful to know, ignorance is learned, the craving to know a kind of madness."[3]

Within these guidelines, let's explore some of the more popular questions generated by the near-death experience.

Does the NDE Afford a Glimpse of Life After Death?

An astounding 75% of the near-death experiencers of The Atlanta Study noted that their conviction of the reality of life after death strongly increased following their NDE, with the rest reporting either somewhat of an increase or no change. These findings are in line with my previous study and with those of others, such as Ken Ring and Cherie Sutherland. Most near-death experiencers felt they had "been to the other side." For them, seeing was believing.

The Bible teaches the reality of life after death. However, when measured against the biblical view, the near-death experience does *not* appear to be an actual glimpse of this afterlife. The author of Hebrews plainly states that "man is destined to die *once*" (9:27, emphasis added), and the wise woman from Tekoa said to King David that at death we are "like water spilled on the ground, which cannot be recovered, so we must die" (2 Sam. 14:14). Both verses yield the same conclusion: once dead, forever dead. Without the direct intervention of God, persons who have died do not rise from the dead back to life again. Thus, if one cannot return from the dead, what a near-death experiencer reports seeing after he returns from his "journey" cannot be, according to the Bible, an early glimpse of the life that follows death.

Jesus further instructed about the nature of death in his parable of the rich man and Lazarus. Here, Lazarus died and was carried by angels "to Abraham's side." An unrepentant rich man likewise died, but was sent to hell. In hell, the rich man "was in torment" and saw Abraham and Lazarus "far away" and implored Abraham to send Lazarus to comfort him with some water. Abraham replied,

"And besides all this, between us and you a great chasm has been fixed, so that those who want to go from here to you cannot, nor can anyone cross over from there to us." He [the rich man] answered, "Then I beg you, father, send Lazarus to my father's house, for I have five brothers. Let him warn them, so that they will not also come to this place of torment." Abraham replied, "They have Moses and the Prophets; let them listen to them." "No, father Abraham," he said, "but if someone from the dead goes to them, they will repent." He [Abraham] said to him, "If they do not listen to Moses and the Prophets, they will not be convinced even if someone rises from the dead" (Luke 16:26–31).

Jesus' teaching is clear: the dead do not report back to the living.

However, several people *were* raised from the dead in the Bible—special cases where the Author of life and death brought life again to one who had died. In the Old Testament, Elijah, through prayer, brought the widow's son who had "finally stopped breathing" back to life (1 Kings 17:17–24). Elisha also prayed to the Lord for the return of the "dead" Shunammite's son, and then performed what could have been an ancient form of resuscitation where he "lay upon the boy, mouth to mouth, eyes to eyes, hands to hands. As he stretched himself out upon him, the boy's body grew warm" (2 Kings 4:34). And when a dead man was cast into the dead prophet Elisha's grave and his corpse touched the bones of Elisha, "the man came to life and stood up on his feet" (2 Kings 13:21).

In the New Testament, Jesus raised three persons from the dead: Jairus' daughter (Mark 5:21–42); the son of a widow in Nain (Luke 7:11–15); and Lazarus, brother of Jesus' friends, Mary and Martha (John 11:1–44). Also, Luke tells of Eutychus, who fell from a third floor window and "was picked up dead." Paul then "threw himself on the young man and put his arms around him" (perhaps an ancient form of resuscitation), and the boy lived (Acts 20:9–12).

In these seven examples, occurring over thousands of years of biblical history, God intervened and returned life to the dead. Clearly, however, these were special events—such reanimations are hardly commonplace today! These were unique situations in which God acted for particular reasons at strategic points in history, usually in the presence of a spiritual leader who sought God's intervention into the normal course of life and death. Interestingly, none of these persons who had been brought back to life were known to describe their brief afterlife experience. Thus, the teaching of Jesus in his parable of Lazarus remains without contradiction; to our knowledge, no one from these events returned from the grave with afterlife details. Accordingly, I conclude that modern-day descriptions of NDEs are not accounts of life after death.

This position, however, leaves us wondering why near-death experiencers' belief in the reality of the afterlife is consistently strengthened following an NDE. If, in fact, they did not participate in life after death, why do they believe in it so strongly? It seems to me that one does not have to *actually experience* life after death to have one's belief in it shored up. The NDE is typically an experience that conforms to the pattern of life after death, and that's why so many return speaking in those terms. It is "afterlife-like," and it is very real. Thus it effectively hints at the existence of an afterlife without actually experiencing it. Some of the issues we examine later in this chapter will tend to confirm this proposition.

If the NDE is not a glimpse into the afterlife, does this mean, then, that the NDE is not a spiritual experience?

Is the NDE a Spiritual Experience?

One of the most consistent features of the NDE is that it is strongly perceived to be spiritual reality both during the experience and later when it is recalled. It contains elements which, when present, conform to a definite sequential pattern (e.g., first an autoscopic out-of-body experience, then entering a tunnel, then seeing a light, and so forth). And when verification is possible, as in the case of Pam Reynolds, these NDE observations are found to be uncannily accurate. All of this suggests that the near-death experience may be something other than a dream, hallucination, or fantasy, which are events perceived in retrospect as being false, which do not conform to a pattern, and which contain diverse and bizarre perceptions of unreality.

In his book, *Essential Truths of the Christian Faith*, popular Reformed theologian R. C. Sproul describes humans as

> creatures made out of a material body and a non-material soul. The soul is sometimes referred to as spirit. Both body and soul are created by God and are distinct aspects of our personal makeup.... At death, though the body dies, the soul of both the believer and unbeliever continues to live.[4]

Professor J. I. Packer calls this soul or spirit the "immaterial personal self" which animates the physical body.[5] It has always been the position of most religious persons, both Christians and those of other faiths, that there is "another world out there," that the material world of the test tube and scalpel is not all that there is. This is borne out by the nearly universal belief in our society in the existence of God, the widespread belief in angels, and the fact that people so quickly turn to prayer when things go badly. This belief in the reality of a nonmaterial world underlies the belief in the existence of the spirit in humans—unlike, presumably, a rose bush or a grasshopper, which are physically alive but lack a spirit. As such, humans can have a spiritual experience where we come in closer contact with the nonmaterial world of the spirit, whereas a plant or other animal cannot.

Scientists have typically avoided dealing with the nonmaterial world and have preferred to operate in the more comfortable world of the physical, which is amenable to examination and measurement. Any study of the NDE, however, brings these two worlds face-to-face and prevents the comfortable partitioning of them. So what we engage in here is in many respects new ground, and I seek to tread carefully in this territory where science and theology intersect.

This spirit of humankind is closely woven into the physical body, making it impossible to cleanly separate the two. This problem arose in Chapter 10, when we examined the NDE and the dying brain. The simultaneous occurrence of an NDE and physical changes in the brain (e.g., the release of endorphins, etc.) did not scientifically establish a cause and effect relationship between these phenomena. And even if a relationship could be established that "proves" that the NDE is a physical brain event, it could well be that God still uses this for his own spiritual purposes. For "How unsearchable his judgments, and his paths beyond tracing out! Who has known the mind of the Lord?" (Rom. 11:33–34)

Belief in the reality of a nonmaterial world, and in the reality of a human spirit as taught by Christianity (and most other religions), creates the possibility that an NDE is indeed a spiritual experience. We are not locked into the necessity of defining it in purely physical and medical terms. In fact, decades of research have failed to yield an adequate physical explanation.

Having been on both sides of this argument, I now believe that the near-death experience is not simply the result of misfires within the dying brain, but that it is a spiritual encounter. Thousands of carefully documented testimonies speak to the near-death experience as being a spiritual experience perceived to be both "real" and "otherworldly." Much of the content of the experience is spiritual. Measurable aftereffects of the NDE, such as an increase in a belief in life after death, in God, and in prayer, weigh heavily in the spiritual direction. And the Bible establishes the reality of such a spiritual realm and our interaction with it.

By saying that I believe the NDE is fundamentally a spiritual experience, I mean four things: (1) it occurs in the realm of the

spirit or soul and not in the physical realm; (2) it is essentially religious in nature and pertains to the things of religion that transcend the material world; (3) it is not amenable to scientific
quantification—no instruments have ever detected and diagnosed
an NDE; and (4) it is real, not imaginary or the product of an
hallucination—experiencers strongly insist that NDEs are not
just another dream. *Bob Guthrie's evaluation!*

I am proposing that spiritual experiences have certain qualities to them and that the NDE possesses those attributes. Here,
the old adage seems to apply: "If it looks like a duck, waddles like
a duck, and quacks like a duck, then most likely it *is* a duck." The
facts of hundreds of NDEs align more precisely with its being a
spiritual experience than any other theory.

This leads us to ask, "But is this experience occurring out of
the body?"

Does the "Out-of-Body" Experience Occur Apart from the Body?

In The Atlanta Study, 26 near-death experiencers described their
experience as if they had clearly left the body and existed outside of it, and 12 additional persons claimed they had lost awareness of their body. Is this really possible? What does it mean to
be out of one's body? To start, we must recognize that the biblical
view of the nature of humankind, possessing both a soul and a
body, does seem to allow for an *out-of-body, near-death* situation.

The apostle Paul may have had a near-death experience
when he was stoned at Lystra and left for dead (Acts 14:19).[6]
When writing of this personal encounter 14 years later, Paul
twice stated for emphasis that he was uncertain whether he was
"in the body" or "out of the body," that only "God knows"
(2 Cor. 12:1–6). Atlanta Study near-death experiencers frequently share Paul's uncertainty. For instance, Greg recalled his
autoscopic experience 26 years later:

As God is my witness, I was out of my body and up by the corner ceiling of the hospital room looking down on the situation. I was trying to figure out how I could do that—be up there and be down there at the same time.... I thought to myself, *Now this is strange.*

Near-death experiencers commonly express this tension between feeling "out of the body" while, at the same time, believing this is not possible by prefacing their NDE descriptions with disclaimers such as "I know this sounds crazy, but...." Both Paul and the modern near-death experiencer seem to be grappling with a similar dilemma that pits their perception of reality against their cognitive understanding.

This dilemma spills over into our scientific evaluation of the NDE as well. Here, independent verification of the accuracy of out-of-body observations, such as Pam's stunningly accurate description of the Midas Rex skull saw used by her surgeon, lends support to the claim that the experience truly occurred apart from the body. But, frustratingly, at the same time, our scientific paradigms are not designed to entertain such a possibility.

As I have considered this conundrum over the years, I now believe that the near-death experience occurs *while* the soul is separating from the body. The spiritual mechanism of death seems best understood as a *process* and not as a single definable moment. This model fits well with our current understanding of the *physical* mechanism of death discussed in Chapter 3, which we also described as a process. Science and religion have much research yet to do on the nature of these parallel processes. While I do not wish to speculate on the details of what these processes are or how they work and interrelate, I believe that the evidence from near-death experiencers comports well with, and points in the direction of, the theory that what occurs both physically *and* spiritually during death are parallel processes.

Following her near-death experience, Charlene grappled with this question. "Was I dead?" she wondered. "Was I really dead? Or was I just in that stage where your body is not completely dead? I don't know that your heart stops and you just die. There has to be a few seconds there in between."

Biblical support for this theory is given in the description of the death of Rachel, Jacob's wife, as she gave birth to Benjamin, recorded in Genesis 35:18–19. Here, Rachel's death was said to occur "as her soul was departing" (NASB), not *when* it departed— *EEG f↓* suggesting that her soul departed over a period of time and not instantaneously. Furthermore, the end of life is said to occur as the soul "withers away, like a fleeting shadow" (Job 14:2), again implying a process. During this dying process, an in-between state may momentarily exist where connection is still maintained with the physical brain (allowing for remembrance of the event if resuscitation is successful) but where the person's spirit or soul is in the process of separation from the body. If the soul continues to depart, death occurs and *physical* memory ceases. If the soul returns, the person revives and may report an out-of-body experience.

There are still mysteries here, as perhaps there always will be with death. How the soul can "see," a physical process requiring *?* the optical mechanisms of the eye, from a vantage point distant from the body is not understood. All we can say at this point is that it seems that the soul is not dependent on the body to accomplish functions we normally think of as requiring physical *Ok* organs and physiological processes. And this is precisely what the Bible says will happen when the dying process is completed and our physical body is gone—the rich man in hell "*looked up* and saw Abraham far away, with Lazarus by his side" (Luke 16:23, emphasis added). *my theater*

Some theologians have addressed this issue of the out-of-body experience using Paul's statements in 2 Corinthians 5:6–8. Here he presented the dichotomy: "as long as we are at home in the body we are away from the Lord," and when Christians are "away from the body" they are "at home with the Lord." Obviously, Paul envisaged life after death where the soul lived on "with the Lord." Biblically speaking, to be "away from the body" is to be physically dead, and from Paul's point of view, with God. Since we have already determined that the NDE is not an experience of life after death, then it would follow that the experience is not truly occurring "out of the body" in the sense that a dead person's soul departs and is irreversibly separated from the body. Paul seems to be considering the two extremes of life and death; in my judgement it is not appropriate to apply this passage to the gray area *between* life and death. Paul's reasoning here does not exclude the possibility that while dying there is an in-between state in which the soul is *separating* from the body—a state which Paul seems to have encountered himself and which left him wondering whether he had been "in the body" or "out of the body" (2 Cor. 12:2).

So we return to the original question, is the NDE an out-of-body experience? It seems that it *is* an experience that occurs as the soul separates from the body in the death process and thus is accompanied by a sensation of being out of one's body, but it is not an out-of-body experience that results from one being dead, for one cannot return from death. If the NDE is so intimately tied to one's soul, it is not surprising that the NDE has been found to cause clear changes in one's spiritual beliefs and religious behavior. These too, may be biblically evaluated.

A Biblical Look at NDE Aftereffects

In comparing the main aftereffects of the near-death experience to scriptural principles, it appears that the NDE promotes, not detracts from, belief in certain biblical principles. It leads to an increase in a belief in God consistent with Paul's instruction in Romans 1:19–20, where he reasons that fundamental divine characteristics are self-evident in the world, leaving people without excuse to reject God. It promotes a belief in life after death that mirrors the words of the wise author of Ecclesiastes when he says that God "has ... set eternity in the hearts of men" (3:11). It encourages one's concern for others, reflecting the words of the psalmist regarding God, who has compassion on all he has made (Ps. 145:9), and the apostle Paul when writing to the members of the church in Galatia, that we should be compassionate and caring for others (Gal. 6:2). It advances one's desire to pray, consistent with the declaration of King David in Psalm 5:1–3 that he prayed daily. And it diminishes one's emphasis on the material world as recommended by Jesus in Matthew 6:25, 33–34 in which he told the crowds in his famous "Sermon on the Mount" to put the pursuit of spiritual matters ahead of material concerns.

These spiritual aftereffects occur across the board in conservative Christians, liberal Christians, and God-believers alike. Biblically, such changes appear to be "good fruit"; and good fruit, we are told, grows only on good trees: "By their fruit you will recognize them. Do people pick grapes from thornbushes, or figs from thistles? Likewise every good tree bears good fruit, but a bad tree bears bad fruit. A good tree cannot bear bad fruit, and a bad tree cannot bear good fruit" (Matt. 7:16–18).

How, then, are these biblical principles so strongly and consistently experienced by people with differing backgrounds and beliefs?

The Revelation of God

God is a Spirit (John 4:24) and is described in the Bible as being "the light of men" (John 1:4) and as a light dawning "on those living in the land of the shadow of death" (Matt. 4:16). Meetings with God in the Old Testament were uniformly accompanied by great fear and a "falling down." Moses met God in the burning bush and "hid his face, because he was afraid to look at God" (Ex. 3:6). In God's presence, Abraham "fell facedown" (Gen. 17:3); Joshua "fell facedown to the ground in reverence" (Josh. 5:14); Ezekiel "fell facedown" (Ezek. 1:28); and so forth. This predictable reaction was not found in the near-death experience. Instead, near-death experiencers felt "loved," "joy," "fearless," "peaceful," "marvelous," "euphoric," "whole," or "pleasant" in the presence of "God." Only rarely were they "in awe" or "humbled."

God further instructed Moses that "No one may see me and live" (Ex. 33:20); and the apostle Paul said that God "lives in unapproachable light, whom no one has seen or can see" (1 Tim. 6:16). As Matthew Henry explains, "The face of God, as involving the full blaze of His manifested glory, no mortal can see and survive."[7]

But claims of "seeing God" are common in NDE reports. Charlene, for instance, saw

> a man standing between the water and me, and he was wearing a brown suit. He had short gray hair, and he was talking, but I couldn't hear what he was saying. He looked stern. . . . I could see his lips moving, but I couldn't hear anything. . . . The man was definitely God. No doubt.

But if the biblical view is true that one cannot directly see God and live, since Charlene lived to describe this encounter, it is doubtful that she and other near-death experiencers reporting similar encounters actually saw the biblical God. They evidently saw a godlike figure whom they understood to be God, but who was not God himself. Thus, the biblical principles enumerated above appear to have been communicated during the NDE through a means other than a direct encounter with God.

The existence of God, along with certain biblical principles, may also be communicated through what has been termed the general revelation of God. This revelation is not a face-to-face meeting with God but an illumination of his invisible qualities—what theologians have called his eternal power, divine nature, and holy law. Such an illumination is a dynamic process whereby God unveils his invisible qualities *to all people* "from what has been made" (Rom. 1:19–20) and *within all people* from divine truths "written on their hearts" (Rom 2:15).

The psalmist declares: "The heavens declare the glory of God; the skies proclaim the work of his hands. Day after day they pour forth speech; night after night they display knowledge" (Ps. 19:1–2). Here, the creation bears witness to the Creator. If God left his imprint on creation in general, then much more should be the case with humankind, who he made in his own image and likeness (Gen. 1:26). A conviction of God "is naturally inborn in all [people] and is fixed deep within, as if it were in the very marrow."[8]

Included in this revelation of God to and within all people is an appreciation of his holy law, for the

> universe reveals something *about him* to men .... [Furthermore,] the moral sense found in all men points us to a moral God who made man in this way. While the precise deeds that men consider right and wrong vary, it seems to be universally agreed that some deeds are right and others wrong.... For example, no society seems to think it right to be selfish. There are differences as to whether a man's unselfishness should be limited to the circle of his own family or extended a little to his own community or nation, or widely to embrace all mankind. But everyone agrees that selfishness is deplorable.[9]

Man attempts to suppress this knowledge in order to escape God's commands. "But no matter how hard we try, we cannot silence this inner voice. It can be muffled but not destroyed."[10]

The universal knowledge received from the near-death experience appears to produce changes consistent with those that would be expected from the general revelation of God; that is, a deepened belief in God and in life after death, an increased concern for others, an intensified desire to pray, and a new emphasis on spiritual matters. This is not new information, however, but a deeper, renewed awareness of that which was already known and which produces, for the most part, feelings of joy and peace—reactions quite unlike the fear and trembling described in the Bible in *direct* encounters with the awesomeness and holiness of God himself.

Thus, I believe that knowledge of God is communicated to the near-death experiencer as part of the general revelation from God. Whether this revelation is mediated through preternatural imagery and spiritlike beings in the NDE as part of God's creation external to the near-death experiencer (Rom. 1:19–20), through an illumination of knowledge which God has engraven on the near-death experiencer's heart (Rom. 2:15), or through both is unclear. My study has led me to conclude that the general revelation of God is occurring in the near-death experience, but it has not allowed me to precisely determine the *means* by which this revelation is accomplished.

Why, then, should this revelation happen during a near-death experience and not at some other point in life? The commentator Matthew Henry states:

> Some of the sweetest communion gracious souls have with God is in secret, where no eye sees but that of him who is all eye. God has ways of bringing conviction, counsel, and comfort, to his people, unobserved by the world, by private whispers, as powerfully and effectually as by the public ministry. His secret is with them (Ps. 25:14).[11]

Furthermore, the psalmist declares, "Be still, and know that I am God; I will be exalted among the nations, I will be exalted in the earth" (Ps. 46:10). The ultimate state of "stillness" short of final physical death occurs during the waning moments of life when heartbeat ceases, breathing stops, and brain waves flatten— a condition nicknamed "standstill" by Pam Reynold's surgeon, who characterized this condition as "nothing, nothing, nothing."

The more we withdraw from the physical world during an NDE, the deeper we enter the "stillness," the more we commune with our heart, the more God and his truth are illuminated within our soul, and the greater the subsequent effect of the NDE on our religious beliefs and activities.

This effect was nicely demonstrated in a little-publicized study of 40 near-death experiencers by Steven McLaughlin and Newton Malony.[12] These researchers scientifically correlated the depth of a near-death experience with change in religious belief and activity and found that the deeper the NDE, the greater the increase in importance of religion and religious activity in the life of the near-death experiencer following the event. The deeper the exposure to God and the further one goes from the mundane physical world, the greater the impact on those beliefs and behavior that reflect a profound inner sense of spiritual truths.

If in an NDE God is indeed revealing himself to the separating soul of a person, then an interesting situation arises when a person who rejects the existence of God encounters a near-death experience. In an article entitled "What I Saw When I Was Dead," atheist A. J. Ayer described such an experience, which he encountered during a cardiac arrest:

> The only memory that I have of an experience, closely encompassing my death, is very vivid. I was confronted by a red light, exceedingly bright, and also very painful even when I turned away from it. I was aware that this light was responsible for the government of the universe. Among its ministers were two creatures who had been put in charge of space. These ministers periodically inspected space and had recently carried out such an inspection. They had, however, failed to do their work properly, with the result that space, like a badly fitting jigsaw puzzle, was slightly out of joint. A further consequence was that the laws of nature had ceased to function as they should. I felt that it was up to me to put things right. I also had the motive of finding a way to extinguish the painful

light. I assumed that it was signaling that space was awry and that it would switch itself off when order was restored. Unfortunately, I had no idea where the guardians of space had gone and feared that even if I found them, I should not be able to communicate with them. . . . I became more and more desperate, until the experience suddenly came to an end.[13]

Ayer remained an atheist following his NDE. He recognized an omnipotent being during his NDE, one who is "responsible for the government of the universe," but absurdly refused to acknowledge God. The light he perceived was red, exceedingly bright, and very painful—radically different from descriptions given by God-believing near-death experiencers. He wanted to extinguish the light, whereas God-believing near-death experiencers desire to embrace the light! Furthermore, he perceived his NDE to be "a badly fitting jigsaw puzzle" where "the laws of nature had ceased to function as they should" (according to Ayer's understanding of these laws, of course); where all "space was awry"; and where he became "more and more desperate" at a time when other near-death experiencers were feeling more and more peaceful. These rather unique characteristics of Ayer's NDE likely resulted from the cognitive dissonance set up between his rejection of God (in the normal mental processes of his brain) on the one hand and the illumination of God in his near-death experience (to and within his soul) on the other.

The general revelation of God not only illuminates God's existence but reveals his laws of existence, which are often suppressed by human wickedness (Rom. 1:18). In the near-death experience, these divine principles appear *unsuppressed*. For instance, persons attempting suicide are in the process of flagrantly violating God's law "Thou shall not kill." During the NDE, however, the suicidal person's desire for death confronts God's moral law and is frequently radically changed. Upon recovery, the recidivism rate of these suicide-attempting near-death experiencers is extremely low, and many go on to counsel others in suicide prevention. These changes are dramatically different from those of nonNDE suicide attempters.

Psychiatrists have studied this effect on suicide attempters and have postulated that during an NDE one feels a "sense of cosmic unity" that causes the person to deemphasize "worldly goals and begin to view his or her individual losses and failures as irrelevant from a transpersonal perspective."[14] This effect of the near-death experience, with its attendant revelation of God, then becomes an effective deterrant from suicide.[15]

In The Atlanta Study, three persons survived suicide-induced NDEs: Jake, Bobby Jean, and Janet. Following these NDEs, Jake repeated his suicide attempt, but Bobby Jean and Janet did not. Interestingly, Jake's score on Hoge's scale, which measures his intrinsic faith and "closeness to God," was 14—one of the lowest in the study; Bobby Jean and Janet scored a 30 and 36 respectively. Exactly *why* Jake's NDE did not produce the otherwise near-universal, deep "closeness to God" found in near-death experiencers is not clear. Nevertheless, these scores align with the above theory. Jake's surprisingly low score, unlike those of the other two near-death experiencers, indicates an extraordinary lack of "closeness to God" which, in turn, left him vulnerable to continued suicidal behavior.

Finally, the general revelation of God carries with it a knowledge of God's retributive judgment (Rom. 1:32). Accordingly, a frightening or "hellish" NDE may represent the unveiling of one's awareness that "there is no one righteous, not even one" (Rom. 3:10), and God's judgment in response to one's condition. This still leaves us with the question of why some people encounter a pleasant near-death experience and others a frightening one. Since, on the whole, frightening NDEs are more frequently reported during blatant violations of God's law such as suicide attempts, it is reasonable to speculate that God's communication to the soul of the near-death experiencer is a confrontation of his or her ungodlike conduct. The negative experience also reflects a higher awareness by the dying person of his or her violation of God's principles for life, and the dissonance between this sense and the felt presence of God. One near-death experiencer reported by Ken Ring had this to say following an apparently "hellish" NDE:

> So I think that God was trying to tell me that if I commit suicide I'm going to hell, you know. So I'm not going to think about suicide anymore [nervous laughter]. (*That did it, then?*) Yeah, I think that did the trick about thinking about suicide.[17]

In summary, near-death experiencers consistently demonstrate a deepened belief in the existence and universal laws of God following their experience—a finding in support of my contention that the NDE involves the general revelation of God. Moreover, this theory is amazingly similar to those proposed by non-Christian researchers such as Ken Ring:

> Isn't it obvious that what core NDErs experience when they come close to death is what the rest of us would call God, or if not God, then surely some aspect of the infinitude of God made manifest to the mind or spirit of the NDEr? . . . If this experience is not of God, then what else could it possibly be?[17]

If Ring, I, and others are talking about a similar relationship of the near-death experience to God, then why do we differ so markedly in other beliefs concerning his Son Jesus Christ, his Word as revealed in the Bible, and in the nature of heaven and hell? John Calvin elegantly explains:

> The manifestation of God [within the general revelation] is choked by human superstition and the error of the philosophers. . . . Surely, just as waters boil up from a vast, full spring, so does an immense crowd of gods flow forth from the human mind, while each one, in wandering about with too much license, wrongly invents this or that about God himself.[18]

Spiritually-charged near-death experiencers and researchers alike can thus be seen to pursue widely differing paths in search of truth and enlightenment—paths which lead as easily down the road to Omega as down the road to Jesus Christ. As with so much of life, the presuppositions we bring to an issue can direct our conclusions.

Is NDE Content Predictive?

Are there differences, then, within these near-death experiences which may signal the spiritual path down which the near-death experiencer will walk?

Using Greyson's NDE Scale (see Chapter 2), the *type* and *depth* of the NDEs were evaluated in each of my three religious groups: conservative Christians, liberal Christians, and God-believers (see Table 5 in Appendix). Four types of near-death experiences were assessed: (1) a "cognitive" experience where mental functions such as perceptions of time, thoughts, and understanding predominated; (2) an "affective" experience where the feelings of joy, pleasantness, and harmony were foremost; (3) a "paranormal" NDE emphasizing out-of-body and ESP components; and (4) a "transcendental" experience in which the entrance into another unearthly realm was most prominent.[19] Using this scheme, the types of NDEs found in each group were surprisingly similar.

Using Greyson's scale, the depth of these experiences in each religious group was also determined and found to be nearly identical.

Finally, the spiritual content consisting of a light, a presence, or a spirit was compared between groups and was likewise found to be similar. Differences did appear, however, in the *identity* ascribed to these spirit-like beings or presences. Christians more frequently identified "Jesus," "Christ," or "Lord"; and God-believers more often "God," "Supreme Being," or "Source." Encounters with "deceased friends or relatives" were more frequently recalled by liberal Christians and God-believers. And "angels" and "Satan" were infrequently named in all three groups.

What, then, can we make of these spiritual encounters? It appears that the content of an NDE is not an infallible predictor of the spiritual path that an experiencer will take. People have free will and take various twists and turns in life and in their spiritual directions. Further, God is sovereign, and insofar as he reveals himself to the near-death experiencer, he will reveal whatsoever he pleases. He is not bound to a formula where those headed for heaven will receive favorable revelation and those headed for hell are further punished with nightmarish scenes. Thus, I do not believe that there is compelling evidence that NDE content or type is an accurate diagnostic of a person's religious beliefs, nor are they road signs pointing to a person's ultimate destiny.

While the NDE does not necessarily predict the final afterlife destination, a frightening NDE may, in fact, be more merciful than a pleasant one, since the "hellish" experience carries with it the warning of God's judgment and, in turn, tends to encourage a turning back to God and a seeking after salvation.

Analysis of the Spiritual Content of NDEs

Within the spiritual realm of the NDE, in which a general revelation of God is occurring, spirit-like entities are encountered. We have already theologically determined that, despite the appearance of these beings, the near-death experiencer is not directly meeting God or the actual spirits of deceased persons (see discussion of the parable of the rich man and Lazarus above). But what about Jesus, the angels, or Satan?

Aside from "God," "Jesus" was the one most commonly identified during near-death experiences in The Atlanta Study. This "Jesus" was intuitively identified. For instance, Dr. George Ritchie, to whom Raymond Moody dedicated *Life After Life,* encountered "Jesus" during an NDE in 1943. "The instant I perceived Him," stated Ritchie, ". . . I got to my feet, and as I did came the stupendous certainty: 'You are in the presence of *the* Son of God.' It was a kind of knowing, immediate and complete."[20]

Betty Eadie, author of the bestseller *Embraced by the Light*, encountered "Jesus" in her well-publicized near-death experience: "There was no questioning who he was. I knew that he was my Savior, and friend, and God. He was Jesus Christ, who had always loved me. . . . I knew that I had known him from the beginning, from long before my earth life, because my spirit *remembered* him."[21]

And Bobby Jean in The Atlanta Study "immediately knew [it] was Jesus. There was never any doubt who it was."

In each of these cases, descriptions of "Jesus" were then given. Ritchie's "Jesus" appeared to him as a "man made out of light" and "a robust male who radiated strength."[22] Eadie described "Jesus" as "the figure of a man . . . with the light radiating all around him."[23] And Bobby Jean's impression was one of "a man figure in flowing white clothing, very bright, and [he had] the most kind, loving look you've ever seen."

Finally, powerful feelings were evoked in the presence of "Jesus." Ritchie felt "unconditional love. An astonishing love. A love beyond my wildest imagining."[24] Eadie was bathed in "the most unconditional love I have ever felt."[25] And Bobby Jean "had never felt that kind of love before, ever."

Thus, in these three cases, the intuitive identification of "Jesus," the descriptions of his being, and the feelings in his presence were virtually identical.

But was this really Jesus? Were they truly seeing the historical Jesus, he who claimed to be one with God?

The Bible instructs that "false Christs and false prophets will appear and perform great signs and miracles to deceive even the elect—if that were possible" (Matt. 24:24). Furthermore, Christ-followers were warned from the beginning: "do not believe every spirit, but test the spirits to see whether they are from God, because many false prophets have gone out into the world" (1 John 4:1). If this is the case, we are faced with the possibility that the "Christs" seen in NDEs are in fact counterfeits, a fact that could only be determined by testing them.

One method of testing was not done: interrogating the spirit as to its identity. The only exception I have been able to find was in a case reported by Maurice Rawlings in which the near-death experiencer met a spirit figure very similar in appearance to the three described above: "a man clothed in a robe that was dazzling white and glowing. His face had a glowing radiance also." As the man approached this figure, he "felt a great reverence" and suspected it to be Jesus. He then asked, "Are you Jesus?" and the spirit replied, "No."[26]

In some instances "Jesus" supposedly passed on messages and instructions to near-death experiencers. Ritchie's "Jesus" allegedly told him of several errors in the Old and New Testament, including the Christian belief that man is a sinful, fallen creature:

> Religion separated from the leadership of God confirms our own negative thinking by telling us we are naked, or inadequate, and fallen sinners.... Unlike the false religions which too often preach a negative identity while serving the Holy Communion (by saying that we are dogs not fit to come to Jesus' table to celebrate the love feast with Him), Jesus came preaching good news.... If God is our Father and Jesus is our brother, then we also have to be gods and not lowly worms.[27]

Eadie's "Jesus" provided her with "absolute and complete" answers to questions dealing with his mission in the world ("His mission was to come into the world to teach love."), with the church ("We have no right to criticize any church or religion in any way."), and with pre-mortal existence ("All persons as spirits in the pre-mortal world took part in the creation of the earth[,]

. . . we knew and even chose our missions in life[,] . . . . [and] we all volunteered for our positions.").[28]

Since these teachings of "Jesus" encountered by Ritchie and Eadie contradict Scripture—something the biblical Christ never did—their "Jesus" is clearly not the same as the historical Jesus of Scripture. Reports of religious teachings received during the near-death experience are very *rare*. In fact, no one in either The Atlanta Study or in my previous investigation claimed to have had such a communication. Furthermore, Ken Ring has raised the possibility that NDE "revelations" may not originate from information "encoded" during the NDE, but may in fact result from "visions" subsequent to the NDE.[29] Ritchie, for example, claimed to have been instructed not only from "what the Christ showed me in my near-death experience but also [from] messages which have come through His guidance and training during the 47 years since my return to life."[30]

In his first book, *Return from Tomorrow*, Ritchie described his NDE as coming to an abrupt end when "Jesus" escorted him back to his physical body. In his second book, *My Life After Dying*, Ritchie claimed that "Jesus" escorted him back and then did

> a startling thing. He opened a corridor through time which showed me increasing natural disasters coming upon this earth. . . . armies marching on the United States from the south. . . . Suddenly this corridor was closed off and a second corridor started to open through time. . . . the planet grew more peaceful. Man and nature both were better. . . . The Lord sent the mental message to me, "It is left to man which direction he shall choose". . . . [31]

Ritchie's addition of this "precognitive vision" to his story is baffling since it is included as a very significant part of his NDE in his second book; but is totally left out of a lengthy presentation of the same NDE published 13 years before. This confusion as to the source and timing of "Christ's" teachings becomes problematic when one considers the reliability of Ritchie's NDE report. One is also left to wonder, *Where did such teachings come from?*

Eadie, moreover, has confessed that "[m]ore experiences have come to me since November 18, 1973," the date of her NDE. At the end of her book, she hints that additional revelations may be unveiled when the time is right.[33]

Bobby Jean's "Jesus," which resembled in appearance and in feeling the spirit encountered by Ritchie and Eadie, did not provide such a message. Following her near-death experience, she chose to walk the path of a conservative Christian, scoring a perfect 11 on the Spiritual Beliefs Questionnaire. Was her "Jesus," then, for real?

Probably not. The Trinitarian view of God, established at the Council of Nicea in A.D. 325 and enjoying widespread ecumenical recognition, holds that there is *one* God which exists in three distinct Persons, and "that each of these three Persons is just God (not parts of God)."[33] Thus, in the gospel of Matthew we are instructed to be baptized "in the name [not names] of the Father and of the Son and of the Holy Spirit" (28:19). The apostle John further reminds us that "there are three that bear record in heaven, the Father, the Word [Jesus], and the Holy Ghost: and *these three are one*" (1 John 5:7 KJV, emphasis added). Since his earthly ministry and the immediate postresurrection period, Jesus figuratively has been seated at the right hand of the Father in heaven (Heb. 1:3; 8:1) and out of sight of the living. Thus, frequent reports of seeing "Jesus" during an NDE, like reports of seeing "God," are most likely not of the Deity himself.

So this leaves us with the angels and Satan. Are they who are seen in the midst of an NDE?

Angels and Satan?

Angels are mentioned in 34 of the 66 books of the Bible, where they are described in some detail: they have intelligence (1 Peter

1:12), emotions (Job 38:7), and wills (Isa. 14:12–15). Although usually invisible, they have the freedom to appear in dreams and visions (Matt.1:20; Isa. 6:1–8), and such visions, not unlike near-death experiences, are predicted to occur in "the last days" (Acts 2:17). They can change shape and appearance at will[34] and can appear as "familiar spirits . . . capable of adopting 'familiar' images and characteristics."[35] This could explain the consistent appearance of deceased persons or religious figures *already familiar* to the near-death experiencer.

Angels are either good or bad. Good angels are termed "elect" (1 Tim. 5:21) and "holy" (Matt. 25:31 KJV). They regularly serve as messengers, comforters, and protectors, and have the particular function of escorting the dead and dying (Luke 16:22). They worship and serve God, and are "sent to serve those who will inherit salvation" (Heb. 1:14).

"Could not the 'rod and staff' which help us in the valley of the shadow of death (Ps. 23:4) be these holy angels?"[36] asks Rev. Billy Graham. I agree with him. The character and activity of the light, presence, and spirit-like figures in these near-death experiences resemble the biblical description of angels.

However, "[w]e have no example in the Scriptures of angels assisting those who doubt God's Word or who refuse to put their trust in God," according to Phil Phillips, Christian researcher and author.[37] Since many near-death experiencers clearly doubt God's Word or at the very least are quite indifferent to it, this speaks against their encountering God's holy angels. But perhaps they are meeting other angels.

Satan and his demons are evil angels with many of the same characteristics as holy angels. However, they oppose God and His servants (Matt. 12:26–28; 25:41) and are commonly thought to present themselves as evil and frightening. Three near-death experiencers in The Atlanta Study perceived such an evil presence in an otherwise predominately pleasant NDE. Ted, a conservative Christian who arrested in the emergency room after suffering a heart attack while mowing grass, was traveling down a tunnel during his near-death experience and approached an opening:

> On the left side of the opening there was just a dark figure, not like a person, not like an animal but like a shadow. It kind of bowed out. You could see over the top and under the bottom and it was just a shadow. It was blocking about one-half of the entrance into that opening. And I could see it move a little bit. I knew something was there, but I didn't know what it was.
>
> I keep wanting to say that that was the devil down there. It was almost like the Lord and the devil were talking it over. The shadow or the black thing sort of overshadowed the opening so you couldn't see into it.

Paige, a conservative Christian, encountered "the angel of death" during her NDE after nearly dying from electrocution in her garage:

> Standing in front of us was a black-robed figure. It was like a monk's robe. I couldn't see his face, but the robe was black. And he had a woven belt and it was a kind of a dull silver pewter. And in that belt there was a silver sword. He was standing there with his arms crossed.
>
> He was standing in front of us over here to our right, and there was a presence standing at my left shoulder. The light from that presence was beaming off that silver sword into my eyes. It's indescribable.
>
> The light which was off that sword had to have been coming from the presence behind me and to the left. Jesus was standing behind me. I said, "Lord, that's not a guardian angel. Guardian angels are very white."
>
> Then all of a sudden I just knew that this was the angel of death. I was very, very frightened. Then I realized that he had

his back toward me. The angel of death was focusing on the presence behind my left shoulder.

And then there was Brendon—a non-Christian, 40-year-old businessman who had nearly died 14 years before while at home one Sunday morning after unintentionally taking an overdose of drugs and alcohol. During his NDE he encountered a door that led into a brightly lit area:

> And from behind the door a figure leaned around, and I couldn't discern any features. All I could see was this black outline of this figure. I saw the right side of the head, the right shoulder, the right arm, and part of what appeared to be a torso down to about the hip. I didn't see any legs. The right arm came up and very slowly made a beckoning gesture to me about two times.
>
> The figure was void of hair. There was no detail of hair, clothes, gowns, nothing. I had no question in my mind where that door was leading me; if I had gone through it, I would have been gone. I have no question about it. It was left up to me to come in.

These three near-death experiencers encountered evil-like spirits who may indeed have been demons. Unfortunately, demons do not always give away their identity by appearing frightening and sinister. Satan, at times, "masquerades as an angel of light" and "his servants masquerade as servants of righteousness" (2 Cor. 11:14–15). These evil angels can "appear extremely appealing, loving and benevolent.... [and] masquerade in order to delude and ultimately to destroy."[38]

This indeed may be the identity of the "Jesus" encountered by Ritchie and Eadie—evil angels masquerading as Christ whose true identity is not recognized by the near-death experiencer's intuition, feelings, or powers of perception. Rather, the being's real identity can be determined only by comparing what it teaches to the Bible. An uncritical acceptance of the identity of godlike figures in an NDE can readily lead to attributing false-hood to God; a more objective measure is needed to assess the veracity of commentary from such "Jesus" figures. Here the Bible is our only reliable yardstick; Paul, in his letter to the churches in Galatia, emphatically warns: "But even if we or *an angel from heaven* should preach a gospel other than the one we preached to you, let him be eternally condemned!" (Gal. 1:8, emphasis added)

Conclusion

After more than two decades of studying the near-death experi-ence, this is where I end up: The NDE is a powerful spiritual experience which causes dramatic changes in one's behavior and beliefs. Without the Word of God, we are without a road map to determine good from evil, and Satan and his demons are free to deceive "even the elect" (Matt. 24:24).

In some instances, "visually observed" events reported by the dying person can be shown to closely align with verifiable reality. The accuracy of these out-of-body visualizations adds scientific weight to the possibility that extra-bodily sight somehow occurred, but from a spiritual standpoint, accuracy *itself* is not a complete diagnostic of godly origin. True "signs and wonders" can also be used by Satan to accomplish his goals (Deut. 13:1–3). Thus, the spiritual message, along with the scientific accuracy, of the near-death experience must be considered.

The underlying message of the near-death experience is con-sistent with the general revelation of God. The near-death expe-rience occurs as one's soul perceives angels in a manner that, physically, humans cannot, for at the point of an NDE, one's soul is partially separated from one's body, being in the midst of the dying process. These angels function as comforters and, at the same time, actively use potent spiritual weapons to guide the near-death experiencer along the path of truth or of falsehood.

In Paul's letter to the church of Colossian believers, he issued this stern warning:

> Let no one keep defrauding you of your prize by delighting in self-abasement and the worship of the angels, taking his stand on *visions* he has seen, inflated without cause by his fleshly mind, and not holding fast to the head, from whom the entire body, being supplied and held together by the joints and ligaments, grows with a growth which is from God (Col. 2:18–19 NAS).

The prize of which Paul speaks is not one's successful resuscitation and return to physical life, but eternal life in the presence of God. And this prize is not received through the worship of the angels, no matter how appealing they may appear, or from taking a stand on a vision during the waning moments of life, but on holding fast to the Head that supplies all that is needed for our growth in God's love and truth.

And this Head is the historical Jesus, the One who proclaimed himself to be the Christ, indeed the very Son of God.

Appendix

TABLE 1

BACKGROUND CHARACTERISTICS OF NEAR-DEATH EXPERIENCERS

	Conservative Christian (22 Persons)	Liberal Christian (13 Persons)	God–Believer (12 Persons)
AGE (Mean Years)	52	54	52
SEX			
Male	36%	62%	25%
Female	64%	38%	75%
RACE	91%	100%	100%
(White)			
EDUCATION	13.4	15.2	14.7
(Mean Years)			
OCCUPATION			
Professional	9%	62%	33%
Clerical-Sales	64%	38%	67%
Laborer-Services	27%		
FUNCTIONAL CLASS[1]			
I	63%	83%	92%
II	32%	17%	8%
III	5%		
YEARS POST-NDE	12.7	15.5	10.4
(Mean)			
PRESENT RELIGION			
Protestant	96%	77%	25%
Catholic	4%	15%	17%
Jewish			
Other or None		8%	58%

TABLE 2

BACKGROUND CHARACTERISTICS OF NON-NDE CONTROL GROUPS

	Group One: Cardiac Surgery Patients (32 Persons)	Group Two: Random Cardiac Patients (81 Persons)
AGE (Mean Years)	62.7	58.6
SEX		
Male	81%	56%
Female	19%	44%
RACE (White)	100%	99%
EDUCATION (Mean Years)	14.5	14.4
OCCUPATION		
Professional	47%	32%
Clerical–Sales	19%	59%
Laborer–Services	34%	9%
FUNCTIONAL CLASS[2]		
I	87%	72%
II	13%	21%
III		7%
YEARS FOLLOWING SURGERY (Mean)	6.2	N/A
PRESENT RELIGION		
Protestant	81%	69%
Catholic	9%	17%
Jewish	6%	9%
Other or None	4%	5%

TABLE 3

SPIRITUAL PARAMETERS

	Conservative Christian NDErs (22 Persons)	Liberal Christian NDErs (13 Persons)	God- Believer NDErs (12 Persons)	Non-NDE Cardiac Patients (81 Persons)
HOGE'S INTRINSIC RELIGIOSITY				
(Mean)[3]	36.1	28.2	25.1	27.8
CHURCH ATTENDANCE[4] (Mean)				
Childhood	1.27	1.23	1.42	
Before NDE	2.14	2.23	3.25	
Present	1.32	2.08	3.17	2.20
CHANGE IN BASIC RELIGIOUS DOCTRINE				
Prior to NDE	27%	15%	50%	
Following NDE	18%	0%	0%	
NON-NDE ASSOCIATED				
Out-of-Body Experiences	9%	15%	17%	9%
Visions	46%	31%	42%	15%
Precognitions	55%	46%	67%	21%

TABLE 4

NET VALUE SHIFTS ON
LIFE CHANGES QUESTIONNAIRE[5]

	Following NDE (42 persons)[6]	Following Cardiac Surgery (32 persons)	
INTRINSIC FAITH CLUSTER	+1.22	+.72	p< .01
Concern with spiritual matters			
Sense of sacred in life			
Inner sense of God's presence			
Religious feelings			
Belief in higher power			
MEANING IN LIFE CLUSTER	+1.17	+.49	p< .01
Sense of inner meaning in life			
Search for personal meaning			
CAPACITY FOR LOVE CLUSTER	+1.19	+.84	p< .01
Desire to help others			
Compassion for others			
Tolerance for others			
Ability to listen to others			
Ability to express love for others			
Understanding of others			
Acceptance of others			
Insight into the problems of others			
INVOLVEMENT WITH FAMILY LIFE	+1.18	+.75	p< .01

TABLE 5

"INDEX" NEAR-DEATH EXPERIENCES

	Conservative Christian (22 Persons)	Liberal Christian (13 Persons)	God–Believer (12 Persons)
NEAR-DEATH CRISIS EVENTS (NDCE)			
Cardiac Arrest	50%	54%	43%
Shock	35%	23%	25%
Accident	5%	15%	8%
Intentional O.D.	5%		8%
Unintentional O.D.		8%%	8%
Other	5%		8%
NDE DEPTH ON GREYSON'S SCALE (mean)			
	13.1	13.8	13.25
NDE TYPE			
Cognitive	4%	8%	8%
Affective	23%	31%	25%
Paranormal	0%	0%	0%
Transcendental	46%	54%	50%
Not Classifiable	27%	8%	17%
NDE SPIRITUAL CONTENT			
Light	59%	54%	42%
Presence	55%	62%	75%
Spirit	46%	39%	33%
None	27%	23%	17%
IDENTITY OF SPIRITUAL CONTENT			
Jesus, Lord	36%	31%	0%
God	18%	23%	50%
Angel	5%	8%	8%
Person	5%	23%	25%
Satan	9%	0%	8%
"Source"	0%	0%	8%
ADDITIONAL NDCEs	32%	8%	58%
ADDITIONAL NDEs	9%	8%	50%

TABLE 6

SPIRITUAL BELIEFS QUESTIONNAIRE

	Conservative Christian (22 Persons)	Liberal Christian (13 Persons)	God-Believer (12 Persons)
1. There is a God			
Yes	100%	100%	92%
Don't know			8%
2. There is life after death			
Yes	100%	85%	92%
Don't know		15%	8%
3. There is a heaven in the afterlife			
Yes	100%	92%	75%
No			8%
Don't know		8%	17%
4. There is a hell in the afterlife			
Yes	100%	46%	25%
No			50%
Don't know		54%	25%
5. The Bible is the inspired Word of God			
Yes	100%	69%	33%
No		23%	50%
Don't know		8%	17%
6. The Bible, written by man, is fallible, and should not be relied upon as literal truth			
Yes		46%	75%
No	91%	17%	17%
Don't know	9%	37%	8%

7. The Bible is inerrant (without error)

Yes	86%	8%	9%
No	5%	54%	83%
Don't know	9%	38%	8%

8. Jesus Christ is the Son of God and thus supreme over all other great religious leaders

Yes	100%	100%	
No			83%
Don't know			17%

9. Acceptance of Jesus Christ as Lord and Savior is essential if one is to go to heaven after death

Yes	100%	38%	8%
No		46%	92%
Don't know		16%	

10. Nonacceptance of Jesus Christ as Lord and Savior condemns one to hell in the afterlife

Yes	86%		8%
No	5%	62%	92%
Don't know	9%	38%	

11. There is a Satan

Yes	100%	69%	25%
No			67%
Don't know		31%	8%

Notes

Chapter One
The Atlanta Study:
A Second Look at the Near-Death Experience

1. R. C. Sproul, *Now, That's a Good Question!* (Wheaton: Tyndale House, 1996), 300.

Chapter Two
Darrell: A Medical and Spiritual Change of Heart

1. Bruce Greyson, "The Near-Death Experience Scale: Construction, Reliability, and Validity," *Journal of Nervous & Mental Disease* 171 (1983): 369–375.

Chapter Three
Death: Defining the Final Frontier

1. As quoted in Robert Truog and James Fackler, "Rethinking Brain Death," *Critical Care Medicine* 20/12 (1992): 1705.

2. The author gratefully acknowledges Dr. Joseph R. Stautner at the Midas Rex Institute in Fort Worth, Texas, for his assistance in supplying information about the Midas Rex bone saw.

3. Linda Emanuel, "Reexamining Death: The Asymptotic Model and a Bounded Zone Definition," *Hastings Center Report* 25 (July-August 1995): 27–35.

4. Madeleine Grigg, Michael Kelly, Gastone Celesia, et al., "Electroencephalographic Activity After Brain Death," *Archives of Neurology* 44 (September 1987): 948–954.

5. Truog and Fackler, "Rethinking Brain Death," 1705–1712.

6. R.C. Wetzel, N. Setzer, J.L. Stiff, et al., "Hemodynamic Responses in Brain Dead Organ Donor Patients," *Anesthesia and Analgesia* 64 (1985): 125–128.

Chapter Four
Survival: Behind the Scenes of a Cardiac Arrest

1. Francis W. Peabody, M.D., "The Care of the Patient," *The Journal of the American Medical Association* 88 (1927): 877.

2. *Matthew Henry's Commentary on the Whole Bible: New Modern Edition* electronic database (Hendrickson Publishers, Inc., 1991).

3. George L. Engel, "Sudden and Rapid Death During Psychological Stress," *Annals of Internal Medicine* 74 (1971): 771–782.

4. Jonathan Leor, Kenneth Poole, and Robert Kloner, "Sudden Cardiac Death Triggered by an Earthquake," *The New England Journal of Medicine* 334/7 (February 15, 1996): 413–419; Yasuhisa Nishimoto, Beverly Firth, Robert Kloner, et al., "The 1994 Northridge Earthquake Triggered Shocks from Implantable Cardioverter Defibrillators," *Circulation*, Suppl.I, 92/8 (October 15, 1995): I–605.

5. Bloomberg News, "Wall Street Tries to Arrest Frequent Heart Attack Deaths," *The Atlanta Journal-Constitution* (December 31, 1997): sec. C, 7.

6. Michael Aminoff, Melvin Scheinman, Jetty Griffin, et al., "Electrocerebral Accompaniments of Syncope Associated with Malignant Ventricular Arrhythmias," *Annals of Internal Medicine* 108 (1988): 791–796.

7. G. L. Engel, "Psychologic Stress, Vasodepressor (Vasovagal) Syncope, and Sudden Death," *Annals of Internal Medicine* 89/3 (September 1978): 403–412.

8. Peter R. Kowey, "The Calamity of Cardioversion of Conscious Patients," *The American Journal of Cardiology* 61 (1988): 1106–1107.

9. B. M. Dlin, A. Stern, and S. J. Poliakoff, "Survivors of Cardiac Arrest: The First Few Days," *Psychosomatics* 15 (1974): 61.

10. Bernard Lown, Regis DeSilva, and Richard Lenson, "Roles of Psychologic Stress and Autonomic Nervous System Changes in Provocation of Ventricular Premature Complexes," *The American Journal of Cardiology* 41 (1978): 979–995.

11. Bernard Lown, John Temte, Peter Reich, et al., "Basis for Recurring Ventricular Fibrillation in the Absence of Coronary Heart Disease and Its Management," *The New England Journal of Medicine* 294/12 (1976): 623–629.

12. P. Reich and P. Gold, "Interruption of Recurrent Ventricular Fibrillation by Psychiatric Intervention," *General Hospital Psychiatry* 5 (1983): 255–257.

13. See Table 5 in Appendix.

14. Bernie S. Siegel, *Love, Medicine & Miracles* (New York: Harper & Row, 1986), 47.

15. Curt Richter, "On the Phenomenon of Sudden Death in Animals and Man," *Psychosomatic Medicine* 19 (1957): 191–198.

16. Clifton K. Meador, "Hex Death: Voodoo Magic or Persuasion?" *Southern Medical Journal* 85/3 (March, 1992): 244–247.

17. K. B. Thomas, "General Practice Consultations: Is There Any Point in Being Positive?" *British Medical Journal* 294 (May 9, 1987): 1200–1202 (emphasis added).

18. Peter Jaret, "The Mind Has the Power to Heal," *Hippocrates* (May 1997): 71–77 (emphasis added).

Chapter Five
Healing: The Power of Faith, Meaning, Love, and Family

1. William Osler, "The Faith That Heals," *The British Medical Journal* (June 18, 1910): 1470–1472.

2. Marvin H. Sleisenger and John S. Fordtran, *Sleisenger and Fordtran's Gastrointestinal and Liver Disease* (Philadelphia: W. B. Saunders, 1993), 409.

3. *Ibid.*, 409.

4. Dale Matthews, David Larson, and Constance Barry, *The Faith Factor: An Annotated Bibliography of Clinical Research on Spiritual Subjects* (National Institute for Healthcare Research, 1993), Introduction. (emphasis added)

5. Gordon W. Allport and J. Michael Ross, "Personal Religious Orientation and Prejudice," *Journal of Personality and Social Psychology* 5/4 (1967): 432–443.

6. Thomas E. Oxman, Daniel H. Freeman Jr., and Eric D. Manheimer, "Lack of Social Participation or Religious Strength and Comfort as Risk Factors for Death After Cardiac Surgery in the Elderly," *Psychosomatic Medicine* 57 (1995): 5–15.

7. Kenneth Ring, *Heading Toward Omega* (New York: William Morrow and Company, 1984) 122.

8. D. R. Hoge, "A Validated Intrinsic Religious Motivation Scale," *Journal for the Scientific Study of Religion* 11 (1972): 369–376.

9. James A. Thorson and F. C. Powell, "Meanings of Death and Intrinsic Religiosity," *Journal of Clinical Psychology* 46 (1990): 379–391. (Note: A slight modification of the wording of two of the questions in Hoge's Scale was used here and in The Atlanta Study)

10. S. Baum, "Age Identification in the Elderly," *Dissertation Abstracts International* 42, (4-B 1981): 1580; P. Fisk, "The Effect of Loss of Meaning on the Mental and Physical Well-being of the Aged," *Dissertation Abstracts International* 40 (1978): 3925B.

11. Jack Medalie and Uri Goldbourt, "Angina Pectoris Among 10,000 Men," *The American Journal of Medicine* 60 (May 31, 1976): 910–921.

12. L. Berkman and S. Syme, "Social Networks, Host Resistance, and Mortality: A Nine-Year Followup Study of Alameda County Residents," *American Journal of Epidemiology* 109 (1979): 186–204.

13. Oxman, Freeman, and Manieimer, "Lack of Social Participation or Religious Strength and Comfort as Risk Factors for Death After Cardiac Surgery in the Elderly," 5–15.

14. Yujiro Ikemi, Shunji Nakagawa, Tetsuya Nakagawa, et al., "Psychosomatic Consideration on Cancer Patients Who Have Made a Narrow Escape from Death," *Dynamic Psychiatry* 31 (1975): 77–92.

15. See Table 3 in Appendix, p < .05.

16. Priscilla was readmitted to the hospital in November 1995 for severe chest pain and congestive heart failure. After cardiac catheterization, it was determined that she was not a candidate for any further surgical intervention. On December 7, her heart failure worsened and she died that night.

17. Richard S. Blacher, "Death, Resurrection, and Rebirth: Observations in Cardiac Surgery," *Psychoanalytic Quarterly* LII (1983): 65.

18. See Table 4 in Appendix.

19. The level of significance of this comparison is p < .01.

20. Kenneth Ring, *Life at Death* (New York: Coward, McCann & Geoghegan, 1980), 133.

21. Ring, *Life at Death*, 171.

22. N. Roewer, T. Kloss, and K. Puschel, "Long-Term Result and Quality of Life Following Preclinical Cardiopulmonary Resuscitation," *Anasth Intensivther Notfallmed* 20/5 (1985): 244–250.

Chapter Six
Prayer: Spiritual Medicine at Work

1. Alexis Carrell, "Man: The Unknown," *Reader's Digest* (March 1941).

2. Yankelovich for the American Academy of Family Physicians, "Doctors Pray for Selves," *USA Today* (March 27, 1997): I-A.

3. Minsun J. Park, "Can Prayer Heal?" *Total Health* 16/2 (April 1994): 22.

4. Randolph C. Byrd, "Positive Therapeutic Effects of Intercessory Prayer in a Coronary Care Unit Population," *Southern Medical Journal* 81/7 (July, 1988): 826–829.

5. Jerry Snider, "Research Support for Efficacy of Prayer: Interview with Larry Dossey, M.D.," *Vital Signs* XIV/2 (Spring 1995): 6.

6. Keith Wall, "Prescription: Prayer," *Physician* (January/February 1994): 17.

7. Editor, "Should Physicians Prescribe Prayer for Health? Spiritual Aspects of Well-being Considered," *The Journal of the American Medical Association* 273/20 (May 24/31, 1995): 1561–1562.

8. Nina Helene, *An Exploratory Study of the Near-Death Encounters of Christians,* diss., Boston University, 1984 (Ann Arbor: UMI Dissertation Services, 1984), 126–127.

9. *Ibid.,* 156

10. Larry Dossey, *Healing Words* (San Francisco: HarperSanFrancisco, 1993), 181.

11. Larry Dossey, *Prayer is Good Medicine* (San Francisco: HarperSanFrancisco, 1996), 44–45.

12. Priscilla was raised Southern Baptist, briefly attended a Mormon church prior to her NDE, and then reverted to Baptist; Abigail was raised Presbyterian (USA), was Presbyterian prior to her NDE, and became Southern Baptist afterwards; Terry was raised Catholic, was Catholic prior to his NDE, and became Presbyterian (PCA); and Wyatt was raised Southern Baptist, was not affiliated with any church prior to his NDE, then returned to the Baptist Church.

13. Greg arrested at home on July 4, 1995 and was unable to be resuscitated.

14. Gary Thomas, "Doctors Who Pray: How the Medical Community is Discovering the Power of Prayer," *Christianity Today* 41/1 (January 6, 1997): 20–29.

15. *Ibid.*, 26.

16. J. I. Packer, "When Prayer Doesn't 'Work,'" *Christianity Today* 41/1 (January 6, 1997): 29.

17. John T. McNeill, ed., *Calvin: Institutes of the Christian Religion* (Philadelphia: Westminster, 1960), 870–871.

18. Editor, "Interview with C. Everett Koop, M.D." *Faith and Medicine Connection* 2/1 (Fall 1997): 4.

19. Sharon Fish, "Can Research *Prove* That God Answers Prayer?" *Journal of Christian Nursing* 12/1 (Winter 1995): 27.

20. Hoge's Intrinsic Religious Motivation Scale score for near-death experiencers with prayer averaged 32.17 and without prayer 29.67 (p = not significant). Within the prayer group, conservative Christians averaged 36.4 and the combined group of liberal Christians and God-believers averaged 27.6 (p < .01).

Chapter Seven
Church: Battleground for the NDE

1. Carol Zaleski, *Otherworld Journeys* (New York: Oxford University Press, 1987), 185.

2. Kenneth Ring, *Life at Death*, 15–16.

3. Kenneth Ring, *Heading Toward Omega*, 252.

4. *Ibid.*, 253.

5. Kenneth Ring, "Psychologist Comments on the Need to Keep Religious Bias Out of Near-Death Research," *Anabiosis: The Journal for Near-Death Studies* (August 1980): 14–16.

6. Raymond A. Moody, *The Light Beyond* (New York: Bantam, 1988), 160.

7. Ring, *Heading Toward Omega*, 145.

8. *Ibid.*, 144 (emphasis added).

9. *Ibid.*, 147.

10. *Ibid.*, 158.

11. Charles P. Flynn, *After the Beyond* (Englewood Cliffs: Prentice-Hall, 1986), 163.

12. Margot Grey, *Return from Death* (London: Arkana, 1985), 107.

13. Flynn, *After the Beyond,* 8.

14. Phyllis Atwater, *Coming Back to Life* (New York: Ballantine, 1988), 117.

15. Cherie Sutherland, "Changes in Religious Beliefs, Attitudes, and Practices Following Near-Death Experiences: An Australian Study," *Journal of Near-Death Studies* 9/1 (Fall 1990): 30.

16. Sabom, *Recollections of Death: A Medical Investigation*, 129–130.

17. Grey, *Return from Death,* xi.

18. Flynn, *After the Beyond,* 6.

19. P. M. H. Atwater, *Beyond the Light* (New York: Carol Publishing Group, 1994), xi.

20. Cherie Sutherland, *Transformed by the Light* (Sydney: Bantam, 1992), forward.

21. Bruce Greyson, "Near-Death Experiences and Personal Values," *American Journal of Psychiatry* 140/5 (May 1983): 618–620.

22. Evelyn Elsaesser Valarino, *On the Other Side of Life* (New York: Plenum, 1997), 112.

23. Amber D. Wells, "Reincarnation Beliefs Among Near-Death Experiencers," *Journal of Near-Death Studies* 12/1 (Fall 1993): 17–34.

24. George Gallup Jr. with William Proctor, *Adventures in Immortality* (New York: McGraw-Hill Book Company, 1982), 192.

25. Raymond A. Moody, Jr., *Life After Life* (Covington: Mockingbird, 1975), 99.

26. Ring, *Heading Toward Omega*, 160.

27. Atwater, *Coming Back to Life*, 151.

28. At the time of interview, 59% of the nonNDE control group of 81 cardiac patients were attending church at the same frequency as 10 years before, 14% were attending more often, and 27% less often.

Chapter Eight
Psychic: More Than Mother's Intuition

1. John Ankerberg, Ph.D. and John Weldon, Ph.D. *The Facts on Life After Death* (Eugene: Harvest House, 1992), 20.

2. Raymond A. Moody, Jr., "Commentary on 'The Reality of Death Experiences: A Personal Perspective' by Ernst Rodin," *The Journal of Nervous and Mental Disease* 168/5 (1980): 264–265.

3. Ring, *Heading Toward Omega*, 182.

4. The difference here between near-death experiencers and nonnear-death experiencers is not significant.

5. Helene, 157.

6. p < .01

7. p < .01

8. John Ankerberg and John Weldon, *The Facts on the Occult* (Eugene: Harvest House, 1991), 22–23.

Chapter Nine
Hell: Uncommon Near-Death

1. Maurice S. Rawlings, *To Hell and Back* (Nashville: Nelson, 1993), 113.

2. Bruce Greyson and Nancy Evans Bush, "Distressing Near-Death Experiences," *Psychiatry* 55 (February 1992): 95–110.

3. Rawlings, *To Hell and Back*, 111.

4. *Matthew Henry's Commentary on the Whole Bible: New Modern Edition* electronic database (Hendrickson, 1991).

Chapter Ten
Scientific Explanations: Nailing Jell-O to the Wall

1. Michael Aminoff, Melvin Scheinman, Jetty Griffin, et. al., "Electrocerebral Accompaniments of Syncope Associated with Malignant Ventricular Arrhythmias," *Annals of Internal Medicine* 108 (1988): 791–796.

2. Ralph Rossen, Herman Kabat, and John Anderson, "Acute Arrest of Cerebral Circulation in Man," *Archives of Neurology and Psychiatry* 50 (1943): 510–28.

3. *Ibid.,* 514.

4. *Ibid.,* 516.

5. James E. Whinnery, "Psychophysiologic Correlates of Unconsciousness and Near-Death Experiences," *Journal of Near-Death Studies* 15/4 (Summer 1997): 231–258.

6. Estrella M. Forster and James E. Whinnery, "Recovery from Gz-Induced Loss of Consciousness: Psychophysiologic Considerations," *Aviation, Space, and Environmental Medicine* (June 1988): 517–522.

7. Whinnery, "Psychophysiologic Correlates of Unconsciousness and Near-Death Experiences," 244.

8. K. Ramabadran and M. Bansinath, "Endogenous Opioid Peptides and Epilepsy," *International Journal of Clinical Pharmacology, Therapy and Toxicology* 28/2 (1990): 47–62.

9. Michael A. Persinger, "Modern Neuroscience and Near-Death Experience: Expectancies and Implications. Comments on 'A Neurobiological

Model for Near-Death Experiences,'" *Journal of Near-Death Studies* 7/4 (Summer 1989): 233–239.

10. Denis Williams, "The Structure of Emotions Reflected in Epileptic Experiences," *Brain* 79 (1956): 28–67.

11. Ernst Rodin, "Comments on 'A Neurobiological Model for Near-Death Experiences,'" *Journal of Near-Death Studies* 7/4 (Summer, 1989): 255–259.

12. Kenneth Ring and Madelaine Lawrence, "Further Evidence for Veridical Perception During Near-Death Experiences," *Journal of Near-Death Studies* 11/4 (Summer, 1993): 223–229.

13. Susan Blackmore, *Dying to Live* (Buffalo: Prometheus, 1993), 180.

14. Wilder Penfield, *The Mystery of the Mind* (Princeton: Princeton University Press, 1975), 73.

Chapter Eleven

Conclusions: The Bible and the Near-Death Experience

1. Doug Groothuis, *Deceived by the Light* (Eugene, Ore.: Harvest House, 1995), 179.

2. P. M. H. Atwater, *Coming Back to Life* (New York: Ballantine, 1988), 135–136.

3. *Calvin: Institutes of the Christian Religion*, John T. McNeill, ed., (Philadelphia: Westminister, 1960), 954, 957.

4. R. C. Sproul, *Essential Truths of the Christian Faith* (Wheaton: Tyndale House, 1992), 133–134.

5. J. I. Packer, *Concise Theology* (Wheaton: Tyndale House, 1993), 74.

6. Charles Ryrie, *The Ryrie Study Bible* (Chicago: Moody Press, 1978), 1766.

7. *Matthew Henry's Commentary on the Whole Bible: New Modern Edition* electronic database (Hendrickson, 1991).

8. McNeill, ed., *Calvin: Institutes of the Christian Religion*, 46.

9. Leon Morris, *I Believe in Revelation* (Grand Rapids: Eerdmans, 1976), 33 (emphasis added).

10. Sproul, *Essential Truths of the Christian Faith,* 12.

11. *Matthew Henry's Commentary on the Whole Bible: New Modern Edition.*

12. Stephen A. McLaughlin and H. Newton Malony, "Near-Death Experiences and Religion: A Further Investigation," *Journal of Religion and Health* 23/2 (Summer 1984): 149–159.

13. A. J. Ayer, "What I Saw When I Was Dead," *National Review* (October 14, 1988): 38–40.

14. Bruce Greyson, "Near-Death Experiences and Personal Values," *American Journal of Psychiatry* 140/5 (May 1983): 619–620.

15. A further implication of this anti-suicide effect of the near-death experience is dramatically addressed in a paper entitled "Last Wish?" by Diane Sabom, Ph.D (unpublished). During physician-assisted suicide, a bystander (such as Dr. Kervorkian) is present to ensure the "success" of the suicide by taking further action (e.g., administering additional drugs or forcibly holding a plastic bag over the head of the person) if, as frequently is the case, the person shows signs of coming back to life once the process has begun. However, the dying person's wish to die often *changes* to a fervent desire to live after consciousness has been lost during an NDE. Thus, the assisting physician or bystander may unknowingly be facilitating death in (or murdering?) someone who is struggling to come back to life after that person has changed his or her initial "last wish" to die to a *true* last wish *to live!*

16. Kenneth Ring, *Life at Death*, 180.

17. Kenneth Ring, *Heading Toward Omega*, 84.

18. McNeill, ed., *Calvin: Institutes of the Christian Religion*, 65.

19. Bruce Greyson, "Near-Death Encounters With and Without Near-Death Experiences: Comparative NDE Scale Profiles," *Journal of Near-Death Studies* 8/3 (Spring 1990): 151–162.

20. George G. Ritchie, Jr., *Return From Tomorrow* (Fairfax: Chosen Books, 1978), 49.

21. Betty J. Eadie, *Embraced by the Light* (Placerville: Gold Leaf Press, 1992), 42.

22. George G. Ritchie, Jr., *My Life After Dying* (Norfolk: Hampton Roads, 1991), 18.

23. Eadie, *Embraced by the Light,* 40.

24. Ritchie, *Return From Tomorrow*, 49.

25. Eadie, *Embraced by the Light,* 41.

26. Rawlings, *Beyond Death's Door*, 98.

27. Ritchie, *My Life After Dying*, 139.

28. Eadie, *Embraced by the Light,* 44, 46, 47, 48, 53.

29. Kenneth Ring, "Precognitive and Prophetic Visions in Near-Death Experiences," *Anabiosis: The Journal for Near-Death Studies* 2/1 (June 1982): 47–74.

30. Ritchie, *My Life After Dying*, 55.

31. *Ibid.*, 30.

32. Eadie, *Embraced by the Light,* 147.

33. G. I. Williamson, *The Westminster Confession of Faith* (Philadelphia: Presbyterian and Reformed Publishing Co., 1964), 26.

34. John Ankerberg and John Weldon, *The Facts on Life After Death* (Eugene, Ore.: Harvest House, 1992), 12.

35. Phil Phillips, *Angels Angels Angels* (Lancaster: Starburst, 1995), 286.

36. Billy Graham, *Angels* (Dallas: Word, 1995), 225.

37. Phillips, *Angels Angels Angels,* 47

38. *Ibid.,* 286–7.

Appendix

A Note About "p" Values and Statistical Methods

Throughout this book, a statistical value of probability—a "p" value—is used to compare possible differences in specific observations made between two groups of people. A "p" value of less than .01 (<.01) means that the difference observed has a less than 1% chance of not being a true difference. Stated another way, p <.01 means that there is statistically a 99% chance that the observed difference is a true difference and not one which occurred by chance. The methods used to determine the "p" values in this book are the "Student t-test" and the "chi-square test."

1. New York Heart Association Functional Classification of physical capacity:

> Class I: No symptoms of fatigue, chest pain, or shortness of breath
> Class II: Comfortable at rest but symptoms with ordinary
>   physical activity
> Class III: Comfortable at rest but symptoms with less than
>   ordinary activity
> Class IV: Symptoms at rest

2. See Table 1 for explanation.

3. These scores were determined from questionnaires returned by 96% of conservative Christians, 77% of liberal Christians, 83% of God-believers, and all of the nonNDE cardiac patients.

4. 1 = Weekly or more frequent
>   2 = Once or twice monthly
>   3 = A few times a year
>   4 = Never

5. Each response on the Life Changes Questionnaire was assigned a numerical value: "strongly increased" (+2); "somewhat increased" (+1); "no change" (0); "somewhat decreased" (-1); and "strongly decreased" (-2). The sum of these values in each group divided by the number of persons in the group are the "net value shifts," which were combined into clusters and statistically compared between NDE and nonNDE cardiac surgery groups.

6. Forty-two of 47 (89%) Atlanta Study near-death experiencers returned the Life Changes Questionnaire.